Joseph
My Son • My Guide

Communications From the Baby I Lost at Birth

by

Kathryn Davi-Cardinale

To Annie
always listen to your inner voice
Blessings
Kathryn

Joseph
My Son • My Guide

Copyright © 2012 by Kathryn Davi-Cardinale
All rights reserved. No part of this book may be reproduced or transmitted in any form or by any means, electronic or mechanical, including photocopying, recording, or by any information storage or retrieval system, without the permission of the Author, except where permitted by law.

ISBN-13: 978-1478355922
ISBN-10: 1478355921
CreateSpace, Charleston, South Carolina, USA
Library of Congress No. 2012914459

Cover art, "Ariyanna," Birth of the Soul©
by Deborah Brooks
deborahbrooks.com
Used with permission. All rights reserved

"Gazing Above"
© 1998 by Alison Joy King
Used with permission. All rights reserved

2012

TABLE OF CONTENTS

INTRODUCTION: WHO IS JOSEPH?   1

HOW THIS JOURNEY UNFOLDED   5

CONTACT   17

JOSEPH SPEAKS   31

PATIENCE   41

ENCOURAGEMENT   49

THE PATH EXPANDS   63

A NATION MOURNS   71

THE TEACHINGS BEGIN   85

SEASONS OF LIFE   103

PEACE   113

LOVE AND PURPOSE   121

APPENDIX I: My Answered Prayers   135

APPENDIX II: Beyond Words   139

AFTERWORD   141

GAZING ABOVE, a Poem by Alison Joy King   143

"... a beautiful testimony to a mother's love, and the strong connection, the golden thread, that binds Mother and Son together, even if that child now lives only in her heart and mind. I am deeply touched by Kathryn's courage both to listen to the messages delivered to her and, in turn, to deliver those wondrous messages of love and angelic protection to the rest of the world." — Deborah Brooks, Visionary, Artist, Inspirational Speaker, Author of *"Daddy" An Invitation to Love* (DeborahBrooks.com)

"Kathryn's sharing of her most intimate and sacred communication experiences with her son Joseph deeply inspires and uplifts one's SPIRIT! It encourages being open to new possibilities as each experience plays across the heartstrings of hope, truth and love within. Having personally lost my son Bobby in an airplane crash and, most recently, my beloved husband Bill, I can so relate to the unique and 'heart-oriented' ways each of our precious loved ones chooses to communicate with us!" — Shirley Ruiz-Orlich, inspirational speaker and author of *Journey to High Places: A Spiritual Odyssey* (quantumangel.net)

"Kathryn Davi-Cardinale's trust in her inner life and experience reaffirms for the rest of us the validity of our own unexplainable contacts from the 'other side' of life."
Alfred J. Garrotto, author of *The Wisdom of Les Miserables: Lessons From the Heart of Jean Valjean* (wisdomoflesmiserables.blogspot.com) and *The Saint of Florenville: A Love Story* (saintofflorenville.com) [optioned for production as a feature film]

This book is dedicated to

GOD

my strength and my breath,

my all and everything,

for abundant blessings and miracles in this lifetime

and to

JOSEPH

for showering me with his constant encouragement,

without which this manual of messages

would neither have been started nor completed.

ACKNOWLEDGMENTS

I am indebted to my parents, Sal and Rose Davi, who inspired me to live my faith. They continue to send unconditional love to me and our family from "the other side." My loving husband Sal has shown extraordinary patience as he has come to understand and accept why I was sitting up in bed writing, often at two or three in the morning.

My daughter Cathi had confidence that this book would be published, long before I did. She is truly my mentor. My son Bob has always supported me . . . "Nothing you do ever surprises me, Mom!" My amazing grandchildren, Carrie, Dan, Lauren, and Alison have taught me valuable lessons. Each one is a teacher to me, as is my dear sister, Norma, who lives her life in gratitude.

Earlene Sykes, my soul sister, opened the window for me to explore. Both Joanne Macko and Kay Taylor gave me confidence to continue on my path. I am grateful to another soul sister, Shirley Ruiz-Orlich, for giving me permission to use her heartfelt story; and to my dear friends, Sandi Metzer, Lorene Caulfield, and June Foster, for allowing me to share their beautiful experiences.

A special thank you to my friend, Deborah Brooks, who graciously granted me permission to grace the cover of this book with her magnificent painting, "Ariyanna"—Birth of the Soul©.

Alfred J. Garrotto, my friend, editor, and noted author in his own right, held my hand and guided me through the final preparation and book-publishing process.

With my heart filled to the brim with love, I say, "Thank you," to my clients who have allowed me to be part of their healing journeys at difficult moments in their lives. I am humbled

I am blessed.

AUTHOR NOTE

I received these inspirational writings through "inner dictation" and was told that they are meant for *everyone* and their content was not to be edited.

I believe that these messages can make our lives fuller and help us attain our highest potential. No matter where one is on the spiritual path, these "words" challenge us to be more loving and forgiving. I have been challenged personally to remove doubt, surrender, and accept.

My hope is that you will read each dictation as if it is being spoken to you.

At the end of selected chapters, you will find a Thoughts and Reflections page, suggesting questions for your personal consideration. I invite you to relate the themes and messages in this book to your own spiritual experiences.

My intention is that sharing my story will bring you closer to your spiritual core and further unveil God's purpose for your life.

We walk this path together . . . and I am grateful.

INTRODUCTION
Who Is Joseph?

Joseph—My Son, My Guide

I was the mother of two healthy children. Bob was five, Cathi three. Two years later, I was pregnant but the baby was stillborn. This little soul was a girl whom I named Mary Ann.

A year later, my fourth pregnancy ended suddenly. I began bleeding profusely, and after 24 hours, my doctor determined that he could not save the baby and induced labor.

My other births had been C-Sections, so natural childbirth was a new experience. I went through labor and had to bear down to deliver. The baby lived three minutes. Had today's new procedures been available, my son would have lived.

I felt radiant and exhilarated after the delivery. I thought to myself, *So this is natural childbirth . . . . It's wonderful!*

Even though my baby didn't live, I felt happy and spiritual, as if something mystical had happened. Why I felt so great I can't explain. It didn't make sense.

I wouldn't know the answer until decades later.

There was a Catholic nurse in attendance at the birth. Knowing my religion, she baptized my son, whom I named Joseph.

He was born May 17, 1958, at 3:02 a.m. and returned home at 3:05.

HOW THIS JOURNEY UNFOLDED

Joseph—My Son, My Guide

"I devoured your words when they came. They were my happiness, and I felt full of joy when you made your name rest on me."
Jeremiah 15:16

In 1983, my girlfriend, Earlene, suggested that we do some automatic writing.

James Van Praagh, in his book, *Talking to Heaven*, describes automatic writing as an exercise used specifically for contacting spirit guides and deceased loved ones. He advises entering into a meditative state of mind while lightly holding a pencil in your hand. When you feel an urgency to write, begin without thinking about what you are writing. And don't *edit* what you write. When the energy fades, put down the pencil . . . and see what you have.

I had never experienced automatic writing, but I trusted Earlene, whose intuitive gifts had surfaced early in life. As a young child, she saw colors around her hands and auras around people. On one occasion, she envisioned a fatal bus crash moments before it occurred near her home.

Earlene and I met when Princess Cruises hired us to work on the Pacific Princess. I had been working at a law office for one year and found that it was not my "cup of tea." I was divorced, my children were grown and I was free to explore new horizons. What I wanted was adventure.

In 1977, I went to see a documentary on cruise travel and immediately thought it would be fun to work on a ship. With the support of my children—"Go for it, Mom!"— I contacted all the international cruise lines to see if my years in the retail jewelry trade would qualify me to work in one of their shops.

Princess Cruises responded with a phone call. I flew to Los Angeles and they hired me. Earlene, who worked in the Princess Cruises offices at the time, also dreamed of sailing the high seas. She too was hired to work in the shops. We met at Pier 35 in San Francisco, where we boarded the ship that became known as the "Love Boat," when Aaron Spelling brought his crew onboard to film the TV series.

I was 41 years old.

I am a Catholic woman with a Jewish heart. Earlene is a Jewish woman with a Christian heart. We are both open to all paths that lead to the one and *only* true God. Our spiritual connection was apparent from the start and we became lifelong friends.

The day we began our automatic writing, Earlene explained that she always went into a meditative state and then asked a question. Since she was familiar with this type of communication, I was simply an observer. I asked if I could at least pose the question and she agreed. Earlene and I began by asking God for protection. We lit a candle and Earlene began to meditate, which she is able to do in an instant. With eyes closed, she held a pencil in her left hand (even though she is righthanded). I proceeded to ask the first question.

"Is there a guide here for Kathryn?"

Earlene wrote quickly, YES.

I asked, "Who is here?"

She scribbled, MARY AND JOSEPH.

It didn't surprise me to hear Mary's name. I've had a devotion to Mother Mary since childhood. In her book, *Mary, Queen of Angels*, Doreen Virtue states that Mother Mary is associated with Catholicism, Christianity, and Orthodox traditions, but that she and Jesus were themselves of the Jewish faith and culture. Mary—like Jesus and the angels, and especially God—belong to all faiths, all religions, all paths, and all people.

I asked, "Is Joseph, Mary's spouse, or is it my child?"

The answer was, CHILD.

"What number child?"

When Earlene wrote, FOURTH, I was blown away. She had no knowledge of how many pregnancies I'd had, nor the nature of the births. She only knew that I had two children and a granddaughter at that time. I told Earlene that I wanted to stop, because I felt strange and didn't want to explore any further.

For several years following that experience, the name JOSEPH recurred in my dreams. I sensed that it meant something, yet the possibility that my son was attempting to communicate seemed farfetched. How could this be?

The subject of communication from "the other side" and the paranormal, in general, had always fascinated me. Now that it was happening, I wasn't sure I was ready for it.

I had read that a spirit sometimes presents itself as a cool breeze, and there had been many nights when I was awakened by a cool or cold breeze on the left side of my face or shoulder. I sometimes saw shadows from the corner of my eyes. I would say in my mind, *Thank you for protecting me. I believe you're from God* (at least, I hoped they were). One night, I was awakened by someone shaking my foot, but no one was there.

Another night, when I lay wide awake, I felt so much love in my bedroom. I thought I would burst with joy. It was like hundreds of angels kissing me. Over and over I said aloud, "Thank you for loving me."

In September 1993, ten years after our first attempt at automatic writing, Earlene and I tried again. I asked the same question, "Who is here?"

Earlene wrote quickly, but this time upside down and backwards. We had to hold the page to the mirror to read it (a phenomenon called mirror script). It said, JOSEPH.

I asked, "Do you have a message for me?"

The answer came immediately, LAUGH.

Skeptical and feeling uneasy, I asked Earlene to stop. Reflecting on this later, I believed the message meant, "Lighten up."

Several weeks later, I was sitting on my sofa reflecting on a dream I'd had the night before. These words jumped into my head.

What would it be like to communicate with Joseph . . . my Son, my Guide? Then the thought, *Is this a book?*

The way these words came through me felt so profound that I got up and wrote them on a piece of paper, saving it with all my journal notes.

Five years passed before that spirit energy began to move more consistently.

On December 14, 1998, I woke suddenly in the early hours of the morning. Words flooded in from another place in my mind. I sat up, turned on the light and wrote as fast as they came, with a sense of deep peace and tranquility.

I SEE CLEARLY

I SEE WITH MY HEART

I SEE WITH MY MIND

I SEE WITH MY EMOTIONS

I SEE CLEARLY

I SEE WITH MY EYE

I don't know why 'eye' was singular. Either I had heard wrong or it was meant to mean "third eye." I had a moment of apprehension before these words jumped into my mind:

BE PREPARED FOR LOVE. A MAN IS COMING INTO YOUR LIFE WHO WILL MAKE A BIG DIFFERENCE IN YOUR LIFE.

Joseph—My Son, My Guide

A physical man or a spiritual man?
BOTH

My mind responded: *Every cell in my body welcomes you.* The thought that followed was again, *Is this a book?* Then, *Why did I think that? . . . What's happening to me that I'm receiving this information somewhere outside of myself and yet it's coming through my mind?"*

I needed some reflection time. I hadn't been on a spiritual retreat for over 20 years. I casually mentioned this while having my nails done, and the manicurist mentioned that she was going to a three-day intensive with India's Siddah Yoga Master, Gurumayi Chidvilasananda, over the New Year's weekend. It took only a day for me to consider it, get on the phone, and reserve a space. I arrived in San Carlos, California on New Year's Eve, 1998.

I experienced a wonderful sharing with people from all over the U.S. and the world, who had come to receive Gurumayi's blessing, which she bestowed on those in her presence, and to hear her annual message to the world.

The retreat was peaceful. The gentle ambience allowed all of us from different religions and cultures to focus on the One God, love, and harmony. I came back feeling relaxed and centered.

Note: Siddha Yoga meditation is an ancient tradition. It is a means of spiritual "unfoldment" leading to the recognition and experience that one's own true nature is divine. Through its principal practice, people from every tradition discover within themselves the awareness that we are not separate from God.

℘

As you continue, what you read may sound rather strange. However, even though I didn't know it at the time, this is how it was meant to unfold.

Believe me, I'm a rational and normal person. I grew up in an Italian American family, lived in a small town, worked in the family business, married and had two children, divorced, worked aboard a cruise ship for 15 months, became a Court Appointed Advocate for Abused Children, facilitated fundraisers for the St. Jude Children's Research Hospital and the March of Dimes. I went on vacations, had family barbecues and, above all, enjoyed my four grandchildren. What was transpiring marked out a new territory for me.

℘

For the next few weeks after the retreat, I thought about my path and what this might mean. On January 16, 1999, I decided to call Kay Taylor in Taos, New Mexico. Kay is a nationally recognized intuitive guide.
I had met her socially through my good friend, Donna

Joseph—My Son, My Guide

Bloom. I simply picked up the phone and asked Kay if she could tell me anything about the name, "Joseph." I told her I had a sense that Joseph was my guide.

Kay was quiet for a few moments tapping into her own guidance. She responded, "Yes, that is the child. He is your guide. He is a partner in the grief work you do. He is a very light being. He was guiding you even before he connected to the body and has continued working with you. Your inspiration comes from him. He draws specific people to you. You have communicated with him for so long that you don't recognize the difference." At the end of our conversation, she added, "Talk to him."

Wow, I thought. *This is confirmation of what I have felt. It's real now!*

I thanked Kay and acted slightly giddy. I said, "I can't believe a baby I gave birth to many years ago is my guide. This is exciting!"

That night when I went to bed, it didn't seem awkward to say, "Well, Joseph, I guess we're a team. Thank you for helping me."

Thoughts and Reflections

What recurring dream have I had? What might this dream be saying to me about my life?

When did I experience a presence or sensed something that felt real, but that I was unable to explain or understand?

CONTACT

January 17, 1999

3:40 a.m.

I was dreaming of contacting someone by sound, when I was suddenly awakened by a distinct "beep sound" to the right of my bed. It sounded like a pager beep (prior to cell phones). My pager was downstairs in my purse.

I was frightened and said: "If that's you, Joseph, please don't scare me." I began to pray the rosary. As I was asking God for protection, my answering machine clicked on, as if there was a message. But, the phone hadn't rung. The tape rewound itself and then beeped off. Frightened, I turned on the light and wrote this experience exactly as recorded below.

3:48 a.m.

I was very nervous. Heart racing, I lit a candle at the altar in my bedroom and walked downstairs to the living room continuing the rosary. These thoughts went through my mind, *Joseph is just letting me know he is with me. It's only a validation.* I had read that "spirit" often makes itself known through electricity and sound. Many of my grief clients had related similar experiences. I wondered if this related to the message I had received on December 14:

A MAN IS COMING INTO YOUR LIFE WHO WILL MAKE A BIG DIFFERENCE IN YOUR LIFE.

Joseph was both physical because I gave birth to him and now he is in spirit. He is both physical and spiritual. The message I received when I asked the question had been:

BOTH.

The beginning of that message had been:

BE PREPARED FOR LOVE.

Why is my heart pounding? I thought. *It's taken me a long time to accept this Joseph.* I recalled my first automatic writing with Earlene in 1983. Again, the thought popped into my head, *Is this a book?*

I took a deep breath and began to dialogue out loud. Let's make this a mental contact, please!" I didn't want sudden apparitions.

I received the answer, **OK.**

This was different from my own words. It came from

another place within. "Thank you, Joseph. By mental, I mean in my head."

I KNOW.

My mind was racing. *I have to call Kay Taylor. I need help understanding this.* Then, these words emptied into my mind, again, from another place.

YOU'LL BE OK. JUST BREATHE.

I said, "You're funny, Joseph." I couldn't help but think, *How can I be afraid of a soul I carried within me?* Then, still holding my rosary beads, I started conversing with Joseph.

Please don't give me more contact than I can handle.. Let's continue to do God's work as a team. I guess that's what you've been doing all along. Be patient with me through this new process of communication.

I felt slightly calmer now. I thanked Mother Mary for helping me through this new experience. I've always felt close to her.

I was still uneasy about going upstairs to check out the blinking answering machine, but decided to do it. The machine still blinked, as it does when there is a message. I decided to wait until daybreak before pushing Play.

At 5:30 a.m., I went back downstairs and watched two Catholic Masses back to back on TV, one in English, the other in Spanish. Now, I was ready to go back upstairs. I pressed Play on the answering machine. It spun and clicked off. No messages.

I thought about this all day. Had I imagined it? No, it really happened.

The next morning at 4:10 a.m., I was awakened again by a beep. This time it came from the hall outside my bedroom. Thirty seconds later, my answering machine did the same thing as the morning before. It sounded like it was recording, then the beeping ceased and the machine started to blink. I felt anxious, but I prayed and stayed in bed.

I said out loud, "I have to sleep," and I did, on and off. At one point, I sat up and wrote, *MY SON AND MY GUIDE*. It was uncanny and awesome at the same time remembering that I had written those very same words sitting on my sofa in 1993. In the morning, I pushed Play on the flashing button. It spun and clicked off. Again, no messages.

That night, I said my rosary and asked Mary to keep me calm. I also called on my lifelong friends, St. Jude and St. Anthony, for extra support. These special guys, as I call them, have helped me so many times throughout my life by interceding for me.

Joseph—My Son, My Guide

I know we have a direct line to God and I do pray directly to Our Heavenly Father and Jesus. The only way I can explain it is . . . it's like asking your Mom or your brother to talk to Dad on your behalf. Call it insurance. Catholics do it all the time. Then, I asked Joseph to please respect my wishes. I preferred that he didn't contact me through electronics during the night.
I need my sleep.

As I lay in bed, the words, **SILENT SPACE**, flooded my mind. Silence fell over my room, a stillness I had never experienced. It felt wonderful to bathe in this space.

During the night, I found myself opening my eyes almost in expectation of a beeping sound. None came. For an instant, I heard a faint, almost guttural sound on my left side. I thought to myself, uncertain how I got involved in all this, *All I want is a normal, fun life. I just want to laugh more.* Suddenly, I remembered the automatic writing experience in 1993. The simple message from Joseph was, **LAUGH.**

The next day, I called Kay Taylor and told her of my two nights of unusual experiences. Kay said: "The energy around the contact is playful. Joseph was very excited that you had acknowledged him. He wanted to make contact in a physical way." She told me I had a choice about communication and that I had to tell Joseph what my boundaries were. I told her I had done that the night before, and my request was honored. There had been no beeping sound, and the answering machine did not spin.

Several nights later, I was awakened by what felt like a silent pager vibration at the base of my spine. I opened my eyes and thought, *Is this a dream?* Now I was wide awake and the vibration continued. With all I had read recently, I believed this was *kundalini* energy. Almost every tradition speaks of *kundalini* in one form or another and describes it in its own way. In Japanese, it is KI, in Chinese, CHI.

According to the late Swami Muktananda in his book, *Kundalini—the Secret of Life*, it is the power of The Self, the power of consciousness. I believe my body was responding to the changes taking place within me. I called it a *gift* and just waited for the vibration to stop.

On the 26th of January, I called my friend Joanne Macko in Naperville, Illinois. Joanne was a new, yet "old soul" friend. We had met in Lafayette, California in 1997, where she was exhibiting her beautiful angel paintings at a new gallery. I was deeply impressed when I heard her story.

Early in her career, Joanne had been nationally recognized for her gifted Grandma Moses-like renditions of 1800s-era scenes. Joanne told me she had always been interested in angels, but it wasn't until the summer of 1994 that she was guided to paint angels, using her hands only, no brushes. Her art is now celebrated throughout the world. She was asked to speak at the United Nations at a meeting held by World Citizen Diplomats, where she presented one of her paintings, "World Peace Angel," to Rodrigo Carazo, former president of Costa Rica. Powerful guidance from the other realm is amazing.

It was natural for me to call Joanne and "pick her brain." She shared how she communicates with guides through writing. It was very similar to what Earlene and I had done with our automatic writings.

Joanne said, "Go into a meditative state. Take a few deep breaths, and on a sheet of paper begin by writing DEAR ONE. Then just let the words flow through your mind onto the paper. At first, you'll feel like you're making it up, but as time goes by, you will know that you are getting the information from another source."

I told Joanne I related to this because I had already experienced the words of Joseph coming from another place. I thanked her for helping me to initiate what was to follow.

The next day, I sat down, centered myself, and felt a little silly. Joseph had been talking to me and I had been writing it all down. What was the difference if I tried to initiate the communication—besides being able to set it up on my time, at my convenience?

I told Joseph of my intention to communicate and took a few deep breaths. As Joanne had suggested, I wrote

DEAR ONE on a legal tablet. Within a few moments, the words seemed to flow swiftly from mind to pen to paper.

I LOVE YOU, DON'T WORRY.

TRUST, OPEN YOUR HEART.

YOU ARE PROTECTED AND LOVED BY MANY.

I AM YOUR SON, YOUR FOURTH BORN.

I AM HERE TO HELP YOU. YES, I'M HERE, JUST LISTEN.

THE WORDS WILL COME, YOU ARE ADEQUATE.

YOU ARE A HEALER, BE OPEN, IT'S BEGINNING TO HAPPEN.

YOU ARE READY, RELAX, LAUGH, PLAY, DANCE.

GOODNIGHT. ENJOY THE PROCESS.

I sat back and read over and over what was on paper. At this point, I wasn't certain that I wanted to continue. Three nights later, when I sensed words coming through. I sat down and wrote:

WE ARE ONE, TRUST YOURSELF, RELAX.

YOU'RE TRYING TOO HARD.

LET GO, LET GOD.

GO PLAY, BE LIGHT.

I took some time to review and reflect on all that had happened to me during the last few days. I thanked Joseph for working with me, but I missed the physical connection through the answering machine.

A couple of nights later, I went to a meeting about helping the homeless, who would be hosted by our parish church in the coming weeks. When I came home, my answering machine was blinking very slowly. When I pressed Play, it rewound. No message. I knew it was Joseph and thanked him for the contact.

Two weeks later, I sat down to make contact again. I hadn't heard from Joseph and hadn't taken time to meditate. Although this new part of my life occupied much of my thinking, I still needed to balance my life.

Mom, who had Alzheimer's, was living with me. I also worked with grief clients and shared time with family and friends.

This is what came through after I moved into a quiet meditative state:

SWEET CHILD, I LOVE YOU, I ALIGN WITH YOU.

WORDS AREN'T NECESSARY.

WE HAVE A HEART CONNECTION.

I asked, "Joseph, are you from God?"

YES, ALL IS GOD.

Thoughts and Reflections

When have I experienced something that I felt was "out of the norm" ... something I wasn't sure really happened, yet *knew* it did?

With whom did I share that experience? If I didn't share it with anyone, why?

JOSEPH SPEAKS

The messages started coming more frequently in the days that followed. Sometimes, I initiated our communication. More often, Joseph alerted me:

JUST TRUST, ACCEPT, BE FREE, LIVE FREE.

LET EACH DAY FLOW. YOU HAVE MUCH HELP.

One night I awakened with my whole body vibrating from head to toe. It was as if my body was a pager, vibrating in silent mode. I asked for a message, and these words spilled out:

YOU HAVE WORK TO DO, BIG WORK.

"Will I have help?"

YES, MANY WILL HELP YOU.

So many questions ran through me. For the next several days, a variety of messages came through to help me:

NOW, IMAGINE OR FEEL A VEIL OF LOVE COMING OVER YOU. FEEL THAT LOVE COME THROUGH YOU

AND AROUND YOU. YOU ARE VERY MUCH LOVED. RELAXATION REPLENISHES OUR BODY, MIND, AND SPIRIT.

QUIET THE MIND. MOVE INTO QUIET SPACE.

STAY CENTERED. BE NATURAL. JUST LOVE,

JUST GO WHERE YOU ARE DIRECTED.

WORDS WILL ALWAYS COME. I AM PLEASED WITH YOU.

WE ARE CONNECTED, YOU KNOW ME. RELAX, RELAX, IT'S SIMPLE.

IT'S ALL ABOUT LOVE. JUST BE, JUST LOVE. CONTINUE TO HAVE FUN AND LAUGH.

One night I said: "Joseph, say something in words I wouldn't normally use . . . not that I don't believe you're communicating, but it would make it even more real to me."

MY DEAR ONE,

MUST YOU ALWAYS BE IN CONTROL?

GET LOOSE.

I got it Joseph!

The thought of writing a book would enter my mind. I asked myself, "What will I write? How to recognize a guide?" I didn't have the answer, so I kept com-

Joseph—My Son, My Guide

municating with Joseph and documenting everything as the messages continued:

GO TO THAT PLACE WITHIN THAT IS PRIVATE AND SAFE. ALLOW LAYERS OF UNRESOLVED ISSUES TO ROLL OFF YOU LIKE A WATERFALL, CASCADING DOWN, PEELING OFF.

SURROUND YOURSELF WITH GOOD PEOPLE, GOOD PEOPLE WITH GOOD HEARTS.

At one point, I felt I wasn't a good receiver and said, "Joseph, please don't walk away from me."

I WON'T. YOU'RE LIKE A FLOWER GROWING SLOWLY. JUST TRUST THE PROCESS—I'M ALWAYS NEAR.

YOU ARE LEARNING. KEEP GIVING YOURSELF TIME TO BE STILL. READ, PRAY, LOVE.
I AM WITH YOU.

WE HAVE BEEN TOGETHER MANY TIMES. LOOK WITHIN FOR ANSWERS, NOT WITHOUT. TRUST YOURSELF. YOU KNOW.

WALK THROUGH EVERY DOOR OPENED TO YOU FOR GROWTH AND UNDERSTANDING. LISTEN TO YOUR INNER VOICE, TRUST IT.
YOU ARE LOVED.

and then:

MARY IS THE DIVINE MOTHER.

☙

More messages...

FOREVER YOUNG,
YOU KNOW I AM THE WRITER AND YOU THE RECEIVER.

BUT I GIVE YOU MY HEART.

BEGIN THE BOOK WITH THE INFORMATION YOU HAVE AND THE REST WILL FOLLOW.
IT IS A PROCESS. BE PATIENT YOU CAN DO IT.
I AM WITH YOU. THE MESSAGE IS NEEDED.

IT WILL TOUCH THOSE WHO NEED IT. DON'T CONCERN YOURSELF WITH THAT PART. YOU ARE A CHANNEL OF LOVE, BUT LOVE YOURSELF. YOU ARE MAGNIFICENT. SEE YOUR OWN LIGHT. FOCUS ON YOUR INNER BEAUTY. THAT IS WHAT OTHERS SEE. OPEN YOUR HEART TO ALL WHO SEEK YOU OUT. JUST TOUCH. YOUR TOUCH WILL HEAL.

By now, I was feeling so much love around me that I was sobbing. "Joseph, will you say something different in this book?"

IT IS ALL TRUTH.

EACH EAR HEARS IT DIFFERENTLY.

"Joseph, how did I get so lucky?"

Joseph—My Son, My Guide

YOU CHOSE IT. YOU WILL TOUCH MANY.

THAT'S ENOUGH FOR NOW.

The next day I kept thinking, *Is tonight the night I will get new messages for all to read?* I was feeling obsessed. When had I really decided to do this work?

I read back over all I had experienced to look for answers. An excitement was building in me. *I need a computer*, I thought. *I can't do this by hand.* Three days later, I began writing everything I had documented to this point, not knowing what the rest would contain. I wanted to enjoy this but felt engulfed, overwhelmed. *Is this going to be published? Who's going to read it?*

As these questions filled my head, Joseph jumped in:

THE WORDS WILL COME.

૪

By May 2, I had almost finished documenting all my notes from my journal, notebooks, and odd pieces of scribbled-on paper. After writing it all down, my part was finished. At one point, I looked up and saw a dove sitting on the ledge outside my window, gazing at me. This gave me the feeling that all was going well.

May 3, 9:00 a.m.

Pencil in hand, sitting at my desk, I declare, "OK, Joseph, here I am . . . apprehensive, but ready." I put my pen to the paper and began writing as the words streamed into my head.

DEAR ONE, IT DOESN'T WORK THIS WAY.

SIMPLY BE OPEN.

YOU ARE ONLY A CHANNEL.

I WILL BEGIN WHEN I BEGIN.

I WILL ALERT YOU WHEN IT'S TIME TO WRITE.

FOR NOW, GO ABOUT YOUR BUSINESS.

I went downstairs and ate a bunch of See's chocolates!

Thoughts and Reflections

How do I relate to Kathryn's need always to be in control of her life?

Why do I have such a strong need to be in control of all aspects of my life?

How might my need for control get in the way of spiritual communication?

PATIENCE

It was a waiting game, a lesson in patience; a lesson I needed to learn. These words came one night:

YOU ARE IMPATIENT.

RELAX, WORDS WILL COME.

THE TIME IS NOT.

I couldn't resist asking again what the delay was about. The answer was:

I WANT A CLEAR CHANNEL.

MEDITATE, PRAY, BE QUIET, REFLECT.

PREPARE YOURSELF.

THE WORDS WILL COME WHEN YOU ARE READY.

MOVE WITHIN, TO THE SAFE QUIET PLACE.

SO BE IT.

Weeks later:

PERFECT YOUR MEDITATION.

GET YOUR COMPUTER. LAUGH A LOT.

THIS IS FUN, YOU WILL REALLY ENJOY IT.

THE BOOK IS ALREADY WRITTEN.

THE REST IS SIMPLE.

In July, another part of my life was about to change big time. Someone I had dated in high school and knew from childhood, lost his wife of 44 years. Sal's wife and I were friends when I was a little girl. Our parents had been friends. I heard through a mutual friend that Joyce had a terminal brain tumor. I was moved to visit her and bring her a rosary that I had brought back from Medjugorje, Bosnia and Herzegovina. The beads were blessed during Mary's apparition to one of the three visionaries who still see her daily. These apparitions have been ongoing since 1981. Their message to the world is: return to God and pray for peace. Unfortunately, I didn't have the opportunity to give the rosary to Joyce personally. She passed before I could visit. I sent them to her husband, Sal Cardinale, explaining that my intention was to give them to Joyce, but now I wished for him to have them.

I also mentioned that I was now a grief counselor, and he could call me if he ever felt the need to talk. Sal did call and we renewed our friendship. In a short time, we started dating.

My mother was still living with me and her Alzheimer's was progressing. Also at that time, I was healing from a rotator cuff problem.

During that period, I meditated infrequently and Joseph contacted me only now and then. I missed my encounters with him and would say aloud, "Talk to me."

I received different messages at different times:

YOU HAVE A MISSION, STAY FOCUSED.

THERE IS TIME FOR PLAY, SPIRIT IS LIGHT.

RELEASING AND LETTING GO IS GOOD.

MUCH AWAITS. YOU ALREADY KNOW THAT.
YOU ARE REMEMBERING WHAT YOU CAME TO DO.

ACCEPT—TEACH—ENJOY.

GOD IS ALL, GOD IS EVERYTHING.

"Am I making this up," I asked, still doubting.

START BELIEVING. YOU DELAY THE WORK.

RELEASE—RELEASE.

HAVE FUN, BUT REMEMBER YOUR PURPOSE.

GET BACK ON TRACK, CHILD.

SCHEDULE YOUR TIME FOR PRAYER AND LISTENING.

I AM WITH YOU, BUT YOU MUST HELP.

ALL IS NEW IN YOUR LIFE, PLAN ACCORDINGLY.

IT WILL BE DONE. YOU ARE A GOOD CHANNEL,

YOUR LOVE COMES THROUGH.

YOU ARE A TEMPLE OF GOD'S LOVE.

October came, and I was still trying to get into a routine of meditation.

My life had become fuller. Sal pleasantly occupied more and more of my free time. I shared my path with him, as well as the messages I'd received. He was open but didn't understand it all. Not even I understood it all.

One night I communicated to Joseph that I missed him, and he responded:

I'M HERE. WE WILL BEGIN AGAIN SOON. YOU ARE MAKING TIME. THAT IS GOOD.

TRUTH CAN WAIT. *IT IS TIMELESS.*

Dec 16. One year had passed since I received that first message: **A MAN IS COMING INTO YOUR LIFE, WHO WILL MAKE A BIG DIFFERENCE IN YOUR LIFE.**

I remembered asking, "A physical man or a spiritual man?"—and the answer was: **BOTH**.

※

Well, 1999 had brought both Joseph and Sal into my life—SPIRITUAL AND PHYSICAL.

And, *yes*, each made a big difference!

ENCOURAGEMENT

Joseph—My Son, My Guide

Come to the edge, he said.
They said: We are afraid.
Come to the edge, he said.
They came.
He pushed them . . .
and they flew.

Guillaume Apollinaire

A new year. I was still struggling with this journey of receiving messages from Joseph. I had doubts, but Joseph kept reassuring me. I needed constant validation.

RELAX CHILD, DON'T TRY SO HARD. I AM DOING THE WRITING. JUST LISTEN.

YOUR PART IS SIMPLE. YOU ARE ONLY A CHANNEL. ENJOY THIS. YOU HAVE CHOSEN TO DO THIS. APPRECIATE THE PRIVILEGE AND JUST LISTEN. REMOVE DOUBT. BELIEVE.

ALL IS POSSIBLE WHEN YOU BELIEVE. CHOOSE LOVE,

CHOOSE TRUTH, CHOOSE JOY. IT IS A CHOICE OF YOUR BELIEF SYSTEM.

REMOVE THE WEBS FROM YOUR MIND. SEE CLEARLY WITH YOUR HEART. SEE WITH YOUR SOUL. SEE WITH YOUR MIND'S EYE. SOAR. YOU CAN DO IT.

EVERYONE CAN. GOD HAS GIVEN HIS PEOPLE MANY GIFTS. OPEN YOUR HEART TO EVERYONE BECAUSE EVERYONE IS GOD. ALL IS GOD. EVERYONE AND EVERYTHING IS GOD. ALL IS GOD. REST NOW, CHILD. THAT IS ALL.

I was awakened one night by a loud noise like no natural sound. I can only describe it as a "rush" of energy hitting the wall.

A message followed:

I AM HERE, AND ALSO THE MANY. WE ARE HERE TO HELP YOU WITH THIS ASSIGNMENT. BREATHE LOVE. IS IT NOT WONDERFUL TO FEEL PEACE? IT IS YOUR BIRTHRIGHT TO ENJOY LIFE, SO DO NOT BE ANXIOUS.

IN HARMONY, ONE SEES CLEARLY. THE ANSWERS ARE EVIDENT. STRIVE TO BE AT PEACE WITH YOURSELF AND WITH OTHERS.

KINDNESS IS NECESSARY FOR A PEACEFUL LIFE. *KINDNESS IS TO LIFE WHAT NECTAR IS TO FLOWERS.*

KEEP CALM AND LET YOUR ESSENCE GLOW. WE ARE ALL HERE TO HELP WHEN WE ARE CALLED UPON. YOU ARE NEVER ALONE. THE MANY STAND BY

Joseph—My Son, My Guide

FOR ASSISTANCE.

WHEN YOU SPEAK, SPEAK WITH LOVE AND
KINDNESS. THE BODY RESPONDS TO KINDNESS AND
THE CELLS RESPOND TO LOVE. HEALING IS
AVAILABLE FOR THE ASKING. YOU MUST BELIEVE AND
REMOVE DOUBT. DOUBT KEEPS YOU FROM YOUR
HIGHEST GOOD.

LEARN TO ACCEPT. ALL IS YOURS.
IT IS GOD'S PLAN.
YOU ARE HIS FLOWERS.
BLOOM AND GROW IN THE SUN HE HAS PROVIDED.
RUN AND DANCE IN THE WIND.
BATHE IN THE WATERS OF THE WORLD.

YOU ARE PRECIOUS TO HIM. THE ALL EMBRACES
YOU. HONOR YOURSELF FOR YOU ARE HIS CHILD.
ALL IS GOD. GOD IS ALL. THAT IS ALL FOR NOW.
BLESS YOU, CHILD.

§

YOU HAVE COME FAR. YOU NOW TRUST
AND THAT WILL MAKE THIS VERY EASY.

BREATHE LOVE AND TRUST THE PROCESS.
EVEN IF YOU DO NOT UNDERSTAND.

YOU ARE ONLY THE CHANNEL. LOVE IS ALL.
MANY WILL BENEFIT. PEACE IS AVAILABLE TO ALL.
IT IS A GIFT FROM GOD FOR THE ASKING. TURN
TO THE HIGHEST FOR ANSWERS AND HELP.
YOU ARE HIS CHILDREN AND HE LOVES YOU.

HONOR YOURSELF FOR YOU ARE ALL PART OF THE *ALL AND LOVING CREATOR*. BLESS EVERY MOMENT OF YOUR LIFE. YOU ARE LOVE. YOU ARE LOVED.

THE MANY ARE WITH YOU ALWAYS.

There were many personal messages throughout the year. In November, this message came through, and this time it was *evident* that Joseph wasn't speaking alone. Perhaps, he felt he needed help with this "doubting Thomas."

WE ARE HERE. WE ARE MANY.

YOU ARE LOVED AND HONORED FOR YOUR INTENTION, SO NOW WE CAN BEGIN. CHILD, THERE IS WORK TO DO. YOU ARE HERE ONLY TO RELAY THE MESSAGE. STEP AWAY FROM THE CONTENT AND LET IT FLOW THROUGH YOU.

YOU ARE A PURE CHANNEL. WE WELCOME YOU IN OUR MIDST.

More instructions came with this new group speaking to me.

It was a lot to digest. At times, I felt like I was on a roller coaster. I was living in two worlds. Although I felt apprehensive and stopped initiating contact, Joseph and The Many did not give up on me. I awakened during the night and early morning hours with either a bell sound, a beep, a touch, or some unusual sound in my ear. At that point, dictation began. I'd sit up and write or go to the computer. The keys seemed to type by themselves. On many occasions, I resisted. I'd turn over and go back to sleep. But most of the time, the words were so loud, I had to give in.

These are the instructions I received:

PRACTICE WHAT YOU PREACH. DO NOT JUDGE. EVEN YOUR THOUGHTS NEED ALIGNMENT. RELEASE THOUGHTS THAT DO NOT SPEAK OF TRUTH AND LOVE. EVERY CELL RESPONDS TO LOVE AND IS DISTURBED BY JUDGMENT.

ALLOW YOURSELF TO MOVE BEYOND LIMITATIONS. THIS PROCESS IS ABOUT SOUL GROWTH.

ARE YOU NOT AWARE HOW GOOD YOU FEEL IN THE PEACEFUL PLACE? YOU HAVE A CHOICE . . . DISCORD OR HARMONY.

ALWAYS, YOU HAVE A CHOICE. WE ARE HERE TO REMIND YOU. WE ARE HERE TO SERVE YOU. CALL ON US. WE ARE WITH YOU NOW.

DO NOT QUESTION OR DOUBT. RELINQUISH CONTROL. YOU ASKED FOR THIS ASSIGNMENT. TRUST IT IS FOLLOWING THE DESIRED PATH OF YOUR SOUL. EXPAND YOUR THINKING TO INCLUDE THE UNKNOWN. ALL IS POSSIBLE.

DO NOT SET LIMITS. THE TWO WORLDS ARE ONE.

ENERGY IS RUNNING THROUGH YOU. YOU ARE ABLE TO BE A CONDUCTOR FOR THOSE WHO SEEK THE TRUTH. YOU ARE PROTECTED BY THE LIGHT OF GOD. YOU ARE BEING SHOWN THE WAY. APPRECIATE THE

PRIVILEGE. BLESS YOU, CHILD.

In December, I made a major decision to place Mom in a private care home. She had lived with me for three years, and I just couldn't manage any longer. When she began having trouble adjusting to her new care and living arrangement, I felt troubled and guilty.

Alzheimer's is a terrible disease. It takes it's toll on the caretakers, too. Every year, thousands of people have to make this same heartwrenching decision. Both my body and my spirit were telling me to take care of myself.

I wrote my feelings at bedtime and, in the silence of meditation, this message came through:

DEAR CHILD, THE PATH APPEARS DIFFICULT,
YET, IT IS SIMPLE. LOOK BEYOND APPEARANCES.
EACH SOUL HAS CHOSEN HIS OR HER PATH.
THOSE WHO APPEAR TO BE SUFFERING HAVE
CHOSEN THIS FOR THEIR SPIRITUAL GROWTH.

ALLOW ANOTHER THEIR PERSONAL JOURNEY,
BUT HAVE COMPASSION FOR THEIR PATH.

YOU HAVE WORK TO DO AND THE FREEDOM
TO ACCOMPLISH WHAT IS AHEAD.

YOU ARE LOVED, CHILD.

"May I ask who you are?"

WE ARE THE MANY.

I reflected on my life and how I was drawn to grief counseling.

Mary, the mother of Jesus, has been with me for as long as I can remember. When I was a child of about nine, I was wearing a Miraculous Medal in the shape of a rose.

For those unfamiliar with this Catholic devotion, it began when Mary appeared to a nun, Sister Catherine Laboure, in Paris on July 18, 1830. During a second contact on November 30 of that same year, Mary asked Catherine to design a medal with a certain image of her on the front, along with the words, "O Mary, conceived without sin, pray for us who have recourse to you."

The reverse side bore other images, including two hearts, those of Jesus and Mary. From France, devotion to Mary Immaculate spread quickly to all parts of the Catholic world. The medal came to be known as "miraculous," when many wonderful cures, both of body and soul, occurred while wearing the medal and offering that little prayer.

I recall wearing the medal around my neck while attending a funeral with my parents. A little girl was crying. It was her mother who had died. Feeling sad because of her great loss, I took my medal off and gave it to her.

Was this the beginning of my grief work? It seems that I have always been searching and seeking, uncertain about what I was looking for. Perhaps it was to bring me to this phase of my life—connecting with the "other side."

A couple weeks later, this dictation came through:

SIMPLY BE OPEN AS YOU ARE NOW.

WORDS WILL BE TRANSFERRED THROUGH YOU. YOU NEED NOT BE CONCERNED WITH THE CONTENT. YOU ARE A BRIDGE AND MANY WILL CONNECT WITH THEIR LOVED ONES THROUGH YOU. THIS IS GOD'S PLAN FOR YOUR LIFE PURPOSE. WE HAVE AN AGREEMENT TO HELP AND ASSIST YOU.

WHEN YOU ARE WITH SOMEONE WHO HAS LOST A LOVED ONE, BE OPEN AND WILLING TO SAY SOMETHING THAT ENTERS YOUR MIND. IT WILL BE UNDERSTOOD. DO NOT HESITATE. JUST LET IT FLOW. THE MESSAGE IS NOT FOR YOU. JUST BE WILLING.

REFLECT ON THE TIME YOU FOLLOWED THROUGH AND DID NOT UNDERSTAND, BUT YOUR CLIENT UNDERSTOOD. YOUR WORK HAS BEGUN. THAT IS ALL, CHILD. BLESS YOU AND APPRECIATE THE PRIVILEGE.

Joseph—My Son, My Guide

I'm reminded of a profound experience I had a couple of years ago. I was working with a young woman who was grieving the death of her father. She missed him so much. She was devastated at losing her loving father and protector.

As I was relaxing her with a peaceful visualization, a thought kept pestering me . . . *GIVE HER FIVE DOLLARS*. These words were repeated many times during our session. *GIVE HER FIVE DOLLARS*.

At the end of our time together, I opened my wallet and said, "I don't know why I'm doing this, but I feel I have to give you five dollars, I hope I don't offend you." She burst into tears and said, "My dad always slipped five dollars into my pocket. I'm low on gas, have no money, and didn't know if I would make it home. I can't believe this!"

She was thrilled for the communication. I was totally in awe of the experience. I thought to myself, *Wow! Her dad used me to get a message to her. What a privilege.* I didn't dwell on it and didn't anticipate it happening again. The Many reminded me!

December 30. Another year had passed, and this was the last message for the year:

BE PREPARED FOR LOVE. AN ABUNDANCE OF LOVE WILL COME TO YOU FROM THIS WORK YOU ARE ABOUT TO DO. BE OPEN AND WILLING. THAT IS ALL.

APPRECIATE THE PRIVILEGE. YOU HAVE MANY HELPERS. WE ARE MANY.

THE WORK WILL COME TO YOU. SIMPLY BE OPEN AND WILLING TO BE THE BRIDGE TO CONNECT LOVED ONES. THE REWARDS ARE MANY. THERE IS GREAT JOY IN THIS WORK.

Thoughts and Reflections

What are my questions about the afterlife?

What do I believe about mutual communication between myself and someone on the other side?

How open am I to receiving such communications?

THE PATH EXPANDS

"The spirit is already an inner guest; we have simply been blinded to its presence." Ernest Holmes, *Science of Mind*

Even with all that had transpired, I still continued to question. I was trying. I really was. When these thoughts or doubts would surface, Joseph and The Many would contact me and offer encouraging words. In addition, recent flareups of fibromyalgia had reduced my energy level.

I received this understanding and loving message:

**WE ARE HERE. DO NOT DESPAIR. ALL IS WELL.
THE TIME IS NOT.**

**TAKE TIME TO HEAL.
IT WILL BE DONE IN DIVINE TIME.
JUST BE.**

THAT IS ENOUGH. YOUR PRAYERS ARE HEARD AND ANSWERED.

IS THIS NOT COMMUNICATION?
WE LOVE YOU.
THE MANY

A few night later I was awakened by a "sound" and these words:

WE ARE HERE. WE HAVE ALWAYS BEEN HERE.
YOU ARE LOVED FOR YOUR INTENTION.
DO THE WORK REQUIRED. STAY ON YOUR PATH.

BE OPEN TO NEW EXPERIENCES. ALL IS WELL.
YOU ARE PROTECTED.

IT IS A JOYFUL TIME. ENJOY IT.
RELAX AND LET GO.

∞

I had received an invitation to an evening social at my cousin's home. I planned to go, but I wasn't feeling well and had spent most of the day in bed.

Something kept nagging at me to go, so I crawled out of bed at 5 p.m. and got ready. Once I arrived, I began to feel better and overheard a woman talking about a seminar cruise she had taken with famed medium James Van Praagh and Dr. Brian Weiss, the author of many books on past life regression. It sounded fascinating. I mentioned that I had read most of their books and would love to do something like that. The woman said that she believed they were planning another seminar cruise in Europe.

That night, I couldn't get it out of my mind. I went to the Internet and googled James Van Praagh. There it was on his website: "voyage of enlightenment." I read all the details and knew I had to go. The two men had chartered one of the Windstar ships to sail around Turkey and the Greek Isles, with a 140-passenger limit. The trip deadline was June 6th and this was already the twenty-second of July! Departure date was August 23.

I closed my eyes and asked God to let every door open easily, if I was meant to go on this trip. The booking agent informed me that a few cabins remained unsold.

Knowing Earlene would like to go, I called her. She said, "Yes, I'll go." The World Airways charter deadline had been extended, so all doors opened wide. The night before I was to leave on my spiritual adventure, I climbed into bed and glanced at the clock—11:11.

℘

It was indeed a voyage to remember. I was delighted to see the name of the vessel when we arrived— *THE WIND SPIRIT.* That evening in the lounge, James Van Praagh and Dr. Brian Weiss gave a welcome talk.

Then, we proceeded to the dining room for introductions around each table. It intrigued me that so many people from different countries had come to be part of this spiritual adventure (India, England, Kuwait, Japan, Canada, Italy, Mexico, Ecuador, and Puerto Rico, in addition to many from all parts of the United States). Every day, before or after port, we had a two-hour seminar with either James or Brian. On a sea day, we had two seminars.

I had written to Joseph in my journal, "Please communicate with me." I was missing contact. The following day, I wrote again, "Please *acknowledge* me—talk to me."

A half-hour later, it was time to go upstairs to the lounge for another seminar with James. I was anxious to hear who would be contacted. So many had already received personal messages from loved ones.

James began by explaining how he worked, saying that he had no control over which spirits came through.

During the first half-hour, he was able to give messages to three people who welcomed communication. It amazed me how specific and personal the information was for those receiving it.

After the last reading, I heard James say, "Alex or Alexander?" He waited for someone to acknowledge the name. Earlene raised her hand, "Yes, that is my stepfather." Since she was sitting in the front row,

James handed her the microphone.

"He says he is really enjoying the fruits of his labor," James said. He then proceeded with personal messages for Earlene's family, mentioning each person by name. Then, I heard him say to Earlene, "Is there a Kate or Kathryn?"

Earlene said, "Yes, that's my friend."

James added, "Is she still alive?"

Earlene responded, "Yes, she's there," pointing to me in the next row.

We were both startled when James said, "He acknowledges her, says hello."

I was dumbfounded. I had only met Alex three or four times. Earlene and I spent most of the night talking about it. Neither of us could get over Alex mentioning me.

A few days later, in meditation I asked, "Why Alex?" I received these words immediately and clearly in my mind:

BECAUSE WE ARE ONE.

I had asked for communication and received it in a way I never expected. I got my acknowledgement. This incident was even more incredible, because Alex had never believed in an afterlife.

The morning we disembarked was emotional for all. There were lots of hugs and exchanges of addresses and phone numbers. That trip was about spiritual awakening, and I believe that everyone on the voyage, including myself, went away having received more than they expected.

Earlene and I stayed overnight in Athens before flying home the next day. From our hotel room, we viewed the Acropolis all lit up. It was a magical conclusion to this "voyage of enlightenment." I had made friends who lived all over the world, and I came to understand what I had always felt . . . WE TRULY ARE ONE.

We arrived home on the evening of September 1, 2001. Ten days later . . .

A NATION MOURNS

Joseph—My Son, My Guide

Our hearts are pierced as we witness devastation on our land. On September 11, 2001, in an act of terrorism, the innocent are taken from us. The world weeps with us as almost 3,000 men, women, and children leave the planet at the hands of ruthless people.

I prayed, wept, and watched TV as it unfolded.
Where do we put this pain? hour by hour . . . day by day.
Numbed by the tragedy, I asked for answers.

Two days later . . .

DEAR ONE, WE ARE HERE. WE STAND WITH YOU TO SPEAK OF PEACE AND LOVE. THERE ARE MANY WHO WISH HARM. TRUST AND PRAY FOR PEACE. THE SOUL ALWAYS KNOWS. BELOVED, GO WITHIN AND SEEK THE TRUTH. SPEAK ONLY OF LOVE. MISFORTUNE OPENS EYES. THERE IS A BALANCE TO "ALL THAT IS."

HARBOR NO ILL WILL, FOR IT SERVES NOT. FORGIVENESS IS THE PATH.

PLACE YOUR TRUST IN GOD. STAND FIRM ON YOUR PERCEPTION. THAT IS ALL. SLEEP WELL, CHILD.

Seven days later . . .

YOU ARE HERE TO LISTEN. MUCH IS HAPPENING IN THE WORLD.

IT IS TIME TO HEAL THE WOUNDS.

PRAY, PRAY, PRAY FOR PEACE. YOU ARE BEING CALLED TO SERVE.

SPEAK OF FORGIVENESS. THIS SOUNDS DIFFICULT IN VIEW OF WHAT HAS HAPPENED. TRUST.

IT IS TIME TO LOOK TO HIGHER GROUND.
ALIGN WITH LOVE ALL OVER THE PLANET.
THAT IS THE STRENGTH AND THE POWER WHICH CAN OVERCOME THIS THREAT OF DESTRUCTION.
SPEAK OPENLY OF YOUR FEELINGS AND VIEWS.

WE STAND WITH YOU. WE ARE MANY. BLESS YOU, CHILD.

I experienced life in a blurred state. The images on TV continued to haunt every moment of the day. I saw blank faces everywhere I went.. Everyone wanted answers.

Four days later . . .

YOUR RESPONSE COMES FROM MANY.

STAND FIRM IN YOUR CONVICTION.

IT IS THIS TYPE OF THINKING THAT CAN SAVE THE PLANET FROM DESTRUCTION.

SPEAK OPENLY OF PEACE . . . THE WORD ALONE IS HEALING.

CAN YOU IMAGINE A WORLD OF PEACE? DO SO, FOR IT IS FROM THOUGHTS THAT REALITY STEMS. STAND TALL. YOU DO NOT STAND ALONE. THE SUPPORT IS HERE, AS MANY RALLY AROUND.

SEND LOVE TO THOSE WHO WISH HARM. "LOVE IS ALL" AND CAN MELT THE HEARTS OF GREED, HATE, AND PREJUDICE.

DO NOT COWER FROM THOSE WHO SPEAK OF REVENGE. *LOVE* IS THE HIGHEST FORM OF STRENGTH. PRAYER IS HEARD. ENCOURAGE PRAYERS AND THOUGHTS OF LOVE. IN THE SIMPLICITY, LIES THE ANSWER.

BEYOND ALL THAT IS SEEN, IS THE UNSEEN, AND IT IS POWERFUL. LOVE YOUR NEIGHBOR, FOR HE IS YOU.
THAT IS ALL, CHILD.

Messages kept coming. In fact, they overwhelmed me. I just kept writing whenever I was alerted. Knowing these messages were to be shared, I began sending them to friends.

WE ARE HERE. WE ARE MANY.

WE STAND WITH YOU TO LET YOU KNOW THAT ALL CAN BE WELL, IF YOU ALLOW IT. YOU HAVE THE CHOICE, AS YOU ALWAYS HAVE, TO STAND FOR A NEW WAY OF THINKING. THE OLD IS NO MORE.

WILL YOU ACCEPT THE CHALLENGE TO MAKE A DIFFERENCE AND SAVE THE PLANET?

CONNECTED, YOU ARE POWERFUL, MORE SO THAN YOU REALIZE. TRUTH IS TRUTH.

LOVE IS TRUTH. BE AS A CHILD AND SEE WITH NEW EYES. GIVE LOVE A CHANCE.

UNITE WITH THE WEAPON CALLED *LOVE*. STAND FIRM. YOU CAN MOVE MOUNTAINS, IF YOU ALIGN WITH LOVE AND PRAYER. BE PATIENT. THERE IS AN AWAKENING. THOSE WHO KNOW, HELP OTHERS TO REMEMBER.
LIVE PEACEFULLY.

BE GENTLE. ALLOW THAT ESSENCE TO FILL THE ATMOSPHERE. IT WILL SETTLE ON MANY MINDS AND HEARTS. PROFESS *GOD IS LOVE*.
STAY CENTERED IN TRUTH.

DO NOT JUDGE. BE A VESSEL OF PEACE AND LOVE THROUGH EXAMPLE.

THIS IS FOR EVERYONE. BLESS YOU, CHILD.
and another . . .

TODAY IS IMPORTANT. BEGIN ANEW, AS EACH DAY YOU HAVE THE OPPORTUNITY TO RETHINK YOUR OPTIONS. PEACE IS THE OPTION. LOVE IS THE OPTION. PRAYER IS THE CHALLENGE.

Joseph—My Son, My Guide

THIS TRULY IS THE "HOLY WAR" AND YOU HAVE THE WEAPONS.

IN THE MULTITUDE IS THE ANSWER. EACH OF YOU IS PART OF THE ANSWER TO THIS CALL FOR UNITY.

and then these words . . .

IF EACH ONE GENTLY PLUCKS A CHICKEN, THE CHICKEN STANDS BARE AND VULNERABLE, BUT NO ONE HAS KILLED THE CHICKEN—AND FOR THIS THE CHICKEN IS THANKFUL.

This same message continued . . .

BE GENTLE IN YOUR APPROACH, BUT STAND FIRM ON THE OUTCOME DESIRED.

IN THIS WAY, THE PLANET CAN BE SAVED.
DO YOUR PART. HONOR AND RESPECT EACH OTHER.
SEE GOD IN EVERY LIVING PERSON,
NO MATTER THE DISTORTION.

STAND ON HOLY GROUND AND PROCEED WITH LOVE.

LET LOVE BE THE WEAPON OF CHOICE.
LOVE IS ALL. YOU ARE PART OF THE ANSWER TO THIS DILEMMA ON EARTH. SEARCH WITHIN AND PROCEED WITH LOVE. IT CAN BE DONE.

NATIONS ARE ALIGNING.

YOUR COUNTRY HAD A WAKE-UP CALL.

ALLOW THIS TO MOVE YOU IN A NEW DIRECTION.

YOU HAVE THE CHOICE TO HEAL OR HURT.
WHICH PATH WILL YOU TAKE?

SHARE THIS IN THE NAME OF LOVE.

GOD IS LOVE—ALL IS GOD.

I couldn't believe all the communication I was receiving, most of it in the early morning hours.

Sept. 30, 2:40 a.m.

YOU ARE HERE TO SERVE. PROCEED WITH
STRENGTH. KNOW THAT WE ARE HERE TO SUPPORT
YOU. WE ARE MANY.

VIEW THE SITUATION AS YOU WOULD VIEW A MOVIE.
OBSERVE. YOU ARE NOT IN THE MOVIE . . . ONLY TO
OBSERVE AND DESIRE A POSITIVE ENDING.

THE MASSES HAVE THE POWER.
PRAYER IS THE ANSWER.

ALIGN WITH ALL WHO ARE OF THE SAME MIND.
SPREAD THE WORD THAT IT CAN BE DONE.
HOLD THE THOUGHT THAT TOGETHER YOU ARE
POWERFUL.

THE UNSEEN IS AT WORK. TRUST.
GO ABOUT YOUR BUSINESS WITH FAITH,
KNOWING THAT THE FORCES OF LOVE ARE
AT WORK. IT CAN BE DONE. MANY HELP.
DO NOT LET FEAR MAKE YOU A HOSTAGE.

LOVE ALWAYS WINS . . . DESPITE THE APPEARANCE
OF CONFUSION AND CHAOS.

I thought they were finished, but a minute later . . .

THERE IS MORE.

DOUBT IS AN ENERGY. BELIEVE ALL IS POSSIBLE, BECAUSE IT IS. LOVE AND PRAYER ARE THE ANSWER.

Concerned about war, I requested an answer during meditation and received this:

YES, IT IS SERIOUS. PRAYER IS NEEDED. ALIGN WITH THOSE WHO WANT PEACE.

THERE IS A CHOICE.

AS WE PROGRESS TOWARD THE GOAL OF HEALING THE PLANET, WE PAUSE TO REMEMBER THOSE WHO LEFT THE PLANET IN A SACRIFICE FOR HEALING. IN DOING SO, THEY UNLEASHED A FEELING OF UNITY AMONG NATIONS.

CONTINUE TO PRAY AND RELEASE YOUR LOVING ENERGY INTO THE ATMOSPHERE.

THIS IS A CALL FOR ALL OF LIKE MIND TO SERVE AND HEAL.

PAY ATTENTION TO WORDS OF REVENGE AND COUNTER THOSE WORDS WITH WORDS OF LOVE. REMEMBER TO PAUSE AND ENJOY EACH DAY OF LIVING ON THE PLANET. SEE THE BEAUTY AND UNITE IN PRESERVING IT.

IT IS TIME TO STAND UP FOR AND PROFESS LOVE OF GOD, LOVE OF ALL LIVING THINGS, FOR IT PLEASES

GOD TO SEE HIS CHILDREN ATTEMPT TO APPRECIATE
HIS GIFTS. ONLY LOVE AND PRAYER CAN ELIMINATE
THE DISASTER OF YOUR PLANET. YOU ARE ALL BEING
CALLED TO SERVE. THE FATHER LOVES ALL HIS
CHILDREN AND WANTS YOU TO LIVE IN PEACE AND
LOVE.
SO BE IT.
THANK YOU, CHILD.
THAT IS ALL.
WE ARE MANY.

On October 12, at 3:09 a.m., I heard the alarm clock and woke up . . . but I had not set the alarm.

This message was even more serious:

WE HAVE COME TO SAY, WE ARE ONE.

WAR IS IMMINENT. PRAY, PRAY, PRAY . . . .
YOU CAN ABORT THE ACTION WITH PRAYER.
MANY WILL SUFFER. A CALL FOR PRAYER IS NEEDED
NOW. TELL YOUR FAMILY AND FRIENDS. PRAY FOR
PEACE.
FILL THE UNIVERSE WITH A CALL FOR PEACE.

THE ENERGY OF LOVE CAN, IN UNISON,
DAMPEN THE THREAT, IF IT IS DONE WITH
DETERMINATION.

MANKIND IS AT RISK. MANY ARE RECEIVING THIS
MESSAGE.
PRAY, PRAY, PRAY.

THE FATHER IS LISTENING. YOU ARE GIVEN A CHOICE
CALLED FREE WILL. LET YOUR ANSWER BE TO SAVE

THE PLANET, IF THAT IS YOUR CHOICE. IT CAN BE DONE WITH MASSIVE PRAYER REQUESTING IT TO BE SO. LOVE CAN WIN, IF YOU CHOOSE IT.

TURN THE TABLE ON EVIL AND REPLACE IT WITH STRENGTH CALLED, "LOVE."

IT WILL TAKE MORE DANGER FOR CERTAIN PEOPLE TO UNDERSTAND. THERE IS HOPE.
GIVE YOUR ATTENTION TO THE SIGNS BEING SHOWN YOU.
IT IS REAL.

SEND LOVE AND PEACE TO YOUR NEIGHBORS ACROSS THE OCEANS.

JOIN HANDS AND HEARTS TO UNITE WITH A FORCE GREATER THAN DESTRUCTION.

LOVE YOUR BROTHERS AND LOVE EACH OTHER.
GOD IS WITH YOU.

BLESS YOU, CHILD.
WE ARE MANY.

I felt totally exhausted when I finished writing.

The next night, I went to bed feeling apprehensive.
Sal and I would be leaving for Hawaii the next morning.
At 2:29 a.m., I woke to these words:

YOU ARE ALLOWING FEAR TO MAKE YOU A HOSTAGE.
IF THAT IS SO, THEN THE ENEMY HAS WON.

IT IS TRUE, THERE IS DANGER, BUT WE HAVE SAID

YOU ALSO HAVE A WEAPON.

PRAY, PRAY, PRAY.
TALK TO THE FATHER.
HE WELCOMES YOUR CONCERNS.

RELEASE YOUR ANXIETY. WE ARE MANY.
WE ARE HERE TO SUPPORT YOU.

THE MESSAGES ARE TO INFORM. GO ABOUT YOUR BUSINESS. ASK FOR STRENGTH, PEACE. IN FEAR YOU CANNOT DO YOUR WORK.
THAT IS ALL, CHILD.

Who were they, these spirits who spoke to me? I had to know. "What do you want to be called?"

RELEASE THE FEAR, RELEASE THE ANXIETY, RELEASE THE DOUBT.

RELEASE YOUR CONCERNS. YOU PUT BARRIERS WITH YOUR LIMITING THOUGHTS.

WE ARE A MULTITUDE OF ANGELIC PRESENCE.

WE ARE MANY.

WE ARE GUIDES, TEACHERS, AND ANGELS.

YOU ARE SO LOVED.
ACCEPT AND BELIEVE.
WHERE IS YOUR FAITH, CHILD?

RELAX YOUR MIND AND LET US COME THROUGH.

YOU MAY CALL OUR ENERGY . . .

Joseph—My Son, My Guide

This seemed like an unfinished sentence, but that was it.

I said simply, "Thank you."

Thoughts and Reflections

What is my strongest memory or image of September 11, 2001?

Where did I find God in the chaos of those days and the aftermath of the disaster?

THE TEACHINGS BEGIN

Joseph—My Son, My Guide

All that followed the 9/11 attack and all the messages I'd received exhausted me. I took a breather and had a hard time regrouping. After meditating one night, I heard yet another message and was taken aback. Because it felt different, I asked questions.

Note: I struggled over including the following exchange, since it's very personal. I chose to share it, because it unveils the startling path that I was called to travel.

DEAR ONE, IT IS TIME TO BEGIN.

"Begin what?"

YOUR LIFE WORK. IT WILL BE REVEALED. YOU ARE READY.

"Who is speaking?"

JESUS

I didn't know how to react. "Thank you," I whispered, confused. It wasn't as if I'd had an exceptional revelation.

Could it truly be Jesus? As I pondered this, I heard these faint words:

YOU STILL DOUBT.

I felt so unworthy and humbled. I still do. As a Christian, I believe that Jesus is the Son of God, one member of the Trinity. That he would speak to me was beyond comprehension. Many who read these pages are Jewish, Moslem, or another religion, for whom Jesus is not considered divine. Rather, they praise him as a holy man, a teacher, or a prophet.

One of the most beautiful encounters with Jesus comes from Paramahansa Yogananda, a Hindu yogi and founder of The Self Realization Fellowship, with over 500 centers around the world, including many in the United States.

In his book, *Autobiography of a Yogi*, Yogananda wrote:

> One night while I was engaged in silent prayer, my sitting room in the Encinitas hermitage became filled with an opal-blue light. I beheld the radiant form of the blessed Lord Jesus. A young man, he seemed, of about twenty-five, with a sparse beard and moustache; his long black hair, parted in the middle, was haloed by a shimmering gold. His eyes were eternally wondrous; as I gazed, they were infinitely changing. With each divine transition in their

expression, I intuitively understood the wisdom conveyed. In his glorious gaze I felt the power that upholds myriad worlds. A Holy Grail appeared at his mouth; it came down to my lips and then returned to Jesus. After a few moments he uttered beautiful words, so personal in their nature that I keep them in my heart.

This struck me as profound, because Yogananda, who is not a Christian, had such a respect for Jesus that he was blessed with this experience.

෴

I thought about Jesus and wondered what I would say about Him if someone asked:

No matter how Jesus is regarded, this man who lived only 33 years, had an impact on every culture, tradition, and religion in the last 2000 years.

For those of us who are Christians, HE IS THE WAY. For others, he opens a doorway to explore their own spirituality.

This book is not intended to convert you. It is simply the story of my personal journey, delivering messages to you from the spirit world.

℘

Everything was quiet for the next few months. Then, more communication from "The Many":

YOU FLIP FLOP. HOWEVER, THAT IS OK.
UNTIL YOUR FAITH STANDS VERY FIRM, YOU MAY CONTINUE TO DO THIS FOR AWHILE.
YOU KNOW IN YOUR HEART THAT ALL IS WELL.
YOU KNOW THAT AT YOUR DEEPEST LEVEL.

SHOW YOUR STRENGTH TO THOSE AROUND YOU, WHO NEED THAT TYPE OF FAITH. PRAY FOR THE STABILITY TO REALLY TRUST. YOU ARE GUIDED AND PROTECTED. CALL ON US AS NEEDED.
THAT IS ALL, CHILD.

I welcomed this gentle "scolding" and carved out time to meditate and become disciplined . . . again.

The following messages are for *everyone*. (I have included messages directed to me but have content for all. Also, I often share some of my own thoughts to help you understand that this was and continues to be an ongoing process.)

If you are a "highlighter" like me, you may want to make special note of those personal messages that seem to be meant *just for you*. You will know which ones they are.

ON DEATH . . .
THERE IS NO DEATH, ONLY TRANSFORMATION
INTO THE LIGHT.

YOU KNOW THAT. IT IS AN ILLUSION THAT WE DIE.
SPIRIT IS WHO WE ARE, AND SPIRIT IS WHO WE
REMAIN. ALL IS SPIRIT.

EARTH IS A SCHOOLROOM OF ILLUSIONS. SPEAK
ONLY TRUTH AND OF LOVE.

WE HAVE BEEN TOGETHER IN THE PHYSICAL AND
NOW IN SPIRIT. IT IS ALL THE SAME. YOU FEEL MY
PRESENCE, SO DID I DIE? DO YOU NOT FEEL YOUR
FATHER'S PRESENCE? IS HE NOT WITH YOU WHEN
YOU CALL UPON HIM? CHANGE THE WORD "DIE"
TO TRANSFORMATION.

TEACH LOVE, BE LOVE. THAT IS ALL THERE IS ON
EITHER SIDE. ATTEND TO THE DYING, AS YOU CALL IT.
GIVE THEM THE REASSURANCE THAT THEY LIVE ON
IN THE LIGHT.

BE A CHANNEL OF TRUTH AND HOPE TO THOSE IN
THE DARK. APPRECIATE THE PRIVILEGE TO SERVE.
YOU ARE A HEALER. TOUCH AND HEAL. YOU WALK
ON HOLY GROUND. ALL IS GOD AND GOD IS ALL.

LET YOUR LIGHT SHINE WHEREVER YOU GO.
LEAD THOSE IN SEARCH OF THE LIGHT.
DO NOT PREACH.
JUST LIVE LOVE.

ON LOVE . . .
THERE IS NOTHING ELSE. LOVE IS ALL. LOVE IS

EVERYWHERE. ONE MUST OPEN THEIR EYES TO SEE IT. IT IS THERE. IT IS IN EVERYONE. EVERYONE IS CONNECTED TO THE ALL, AND THE ALL IS LOVE.

WE WANT YOU TO KNOW THAT ONE CONTINUES TO LEARN WHEN THE SOUL LEAVES THE BODY.

As I've said before, even though this message was directed to me, it's for everyone.

We *all* walk on holy ground. We are *all* healers. As an example, when we hug and comfort, when we tend to the sick, when we touch the hand of a lonely person, isn't that healing? Healing to me is physical, mental, emotional, and spiritual.

We are *all* here to serve. We *all* have God within. We are love. We are *all* connected, and the connection doesn't end. I believe that contact with a loved one after death can and does happen, when you are open and ready to receive it.

Friends and clients have given me permission to share their experiences. I will also include some of my own. I'm sure that many of you reading this have your own experiences that you may have doubted or thought were your imagination. I've been there. I understand. I have doubted . . . and still do at times.

I'm glad to know that we continue learning after we "cross over." I still have a lot to learn.

I was exceptionally sad, hearing of a tragic accident in which a friend's husband was killed. Earth life is so fragile. I meditated, prayed, and asked for words from my guides.

WE ARE HERE AS YOU REQUESTED.
SIMPLY BE OPEN TO WHAT FLOWS THROUGH YOU.
YES, THE PATH CAN BE DIFFICULT, AND YET THIS
IS WHAT LIFE ON EARTH IS ABOUT.
EACH SOUL MAKES THIS ARRANGEMENT PRIOR
TO COMING TO EARTH.

THE LESSONS ARE FOR SOUL GROWTH. LOVE
CONTINUES, HOWEVER, AS THE VEIL IS THIN AND
BOTH WORLDS CONNECT. YOU CAN SENSE THE
PRESENCE OF A LOVED ONE SIMPLY BY WISHING
IT AND ASKING FOR THE COMMUNICATION. BE AWARE
THAT COMMUNICATION COMES IN MANY FORMS.
WHEN IT IS TIME, YOU CAN HELP WITH
THE CONNECTIONS. MANY SUPPORT YOU.
YOU ARE NEVER ALONE.

TRUST THAT WE WILL ALWAYS BE HELPERS IN YOUR
WORK. THIS IS AN AGREEMENT WE HAVE MADE
TOGETHER. LET LOVE BE THE THREAD
THAT CONNECTS THE VIBRATION. LET IT FLOW
THROUGH YOU WITHOUT EFFORT. THIS IS A UNION
OF LOVE. SIMPLY LOVE AND TRUST AND ENJOY THE
GIFT YOU HAVE TO OFFER.

APPRECIATE THE PRIVILEGE.

One night I was thinking of young children and young adults who have died too soon and the heartbreak felt by their parents. I have had clients and friends who have lost children to accidents, illness, or violence.

I'm reminded of my good friend, Shirley Ruiz-Orlich, whom I've known since high school. Shirley's son, Bobby, died when the cargo plane he was piloting crashed into Mt. Shasta, in California. Shirley was propelled to begin a spiritual quest in an effort to make sense of this horrific loss. She traveled the world in pursuit of answers. Her book, *Journey to High Places*, has been a comfort and a healing source to other parents who have lost children.

In her book, Shirley mentions going to Puerto Vallarta to celebrate her 50th birthday with her daughter Kim. She was considering going parasailing, after watching Kim go up. She looked in her wallet and only had a fifty dollar bill. Shirley remembered the boys handling the rides saying that they had no change. She writes:

> As I stood there, blank as to what to do, my body trembled as I heard Bobby's voice saying: "Mom, this is my golden birthday present to you. Take my money and come fly with me!" I blinked my eyes in disbelief as I remembered the money that had belonged to Bobby when they had brought

his body down from Mt. Shasta. It had been hidden away in a secret place in my wallet. I'd forgotten all about it after promising myself that I'd know when it was the right occasion to spend it. Flying high with Bobby—of course, this was it. I could hear Bobby talking to me, and as I sailed high above the water, I found myself singing, laughing and crying all in the same moment.

A mother-child relationship knows no boundaries, even if the child lived only three minutes.

℘

Often, I would wake in the wee hours. On one occasion, at 3:15 a.m., my eyes opened and I was wide awake. I knew I had to write since the words were already coming through my mind. When I read it later, I knew this message would touch *many* hearts.

THANK YOU FOR LISTENING.
WE ARE HERE TO SAY ALL SOULS HAVE MERIT.
NO MATTER HOW LONG THEY LIVE ON EARTH.
OFTEN, THE SHORTEST EARTH LIFE ACCOMPLISHES THE MISSION INTENDED.

ONE MAY ASK ABOUT ABORTION. YES, IT IS TRUE THAT THERE WILL BE A REUNION BETWEEN MOTHER

AND CHILD.

EACH SOUL KNOWS ITS PURPOSE AND LESSON.
THE ABORTED SOUL LIVES.
FORGIVENESS IS THE GIFT.

This next message took me by surprise:

THIS CHANNEL HAS BEEN SKEPTICAL FOR YEARS, BUT WE HAVE BEEN PATIENT WITH HER. HOW MANY TIMES DID SHE PUT ASIDE "THE KNOWING" AND DOUBTED OUR CONTACT.

I, JOSEPH, KNEW ALL ALONG THE TIME WOULD COME THAT SHE WOULD WAKE UP TO THE TRUTH OF THIS HAPPENING.

Wow! Talking about me like I was not in the room! A strange journey, indeed.

IT IS OUR CONCERN THAT SOULS ON THE OTHER SIDE, AS YOU CALL IT, HAVE A PORTAL, A PATHWAY TO CONNECT WITH LOVED ONES.
WE WANT THOSE ON EARTH TO KNOW THAT IT IS WITHIN THEIR REACH TO COMMUNICATE.

SIMPLY BE OPEN AND CLEAR THE SPACE FOR COMMUNICATION. MEDITATE, PRAY, AND BE OPEN TO HOW THE LOVED ONE SENDS THEIR LOVE.

OH, HOW SWEET IT IS WHEN THAT HAPPENS. THERE ARE NO BOUNDARIES TO REACH THOSE IN THE AFTERLIFE. IT IS JOYFUL WHEN A CONNECTION IS MADE. ONLY THE SOULS INVOLVED KNOW THE JOY. DO IT NOW.

Joseph—My Son, My Guide

FOR ALL WHO ARE READING THIS NOW; SIMPLY
CLOSE YOUR EYES AND BRING YOUR LOVED ONE'S
FACE INTO YOUR HEART WITH EYES CLOSED.
BREATHE AND FEEL THEIR PRESENCE.

(Pause here to do as The Many suggest.)

DO THIS OFTEN, UNTIL YOU BECOME ONE WITH
YOUR LOVED ONE. TALK TO YOUR LOVED ONE
AND LET THEM KNOW YOU ARE OPEN AND READY
FOR COMMUNICATION THROUGH YOUR MIND,
THROUGH MUSIC, SOMETHING KNOWN ONLY TO
THE TWO OF YOU. A STILLNESS, A BREEZE,
A SMELL, AROMA, COLOR, ANIMAL, OR BIRD.
YOU WILL KNOW IN YOUR HEART THAT YOUR LOVED
ONE IS CLOSE. LOOK FOR THE UNEXPLAINABLE.
THERE ARE NO BOUNDARIES IN SPIRIT.

A LOST ITEM CAN APPEAR OUT OF THE BLUE.
ELECTRICAL DEVICES CAN GO ON AND OFF.
BE OPEN TO HOW COMMUNICATION COMES.

AS WE HAVE SAID BEFORE, THERE IS NO DEATH—
ONLY TRANSFORMATION. THE SOUL NEVER DIES.
THE SPIRIT IS ALIVE AND WELL.

DO NOT FEEL REJECTED IF CONTACT DOES NOT
HAPPEN IMMEDIATELY. BE KIND TO YOURSELVES.
ANXIETY DOES NOT SERVE. CALMNESS, CHILD-
LIKE WONDER, AND PATIENCE ARE NEEDED.
THAT IS ALL. IT IS SIMPLE.
IT'S JUST A BRIDGE TO THE OTHER SIDE. THE VEIL
IS THIN.

ASK FOR HELP. EACH SOUL HAS AN ANGEL AND A GUIDE. WE ALL STAND TO BE ASKED. IT IS SIMPLE.

IT WILL COME IF THE DESIRE IS STRONG. IT WILL HAPPEN WHEN YOU LEAST EXPECT IT. YOU WILL KNOW. IT IS JUST FOR YOU. DON'T SECOND-GUESS THE EXPERIENCE.
YOU WILL KNOW.
REJOICE IN THE CONNECTION.

☙

I will relate here a precious story. The daughter of my good friend Lorene died at too early an age. At the cemetery, about 25 family members, including the deceased's husband, were given butterflies to release at a certain time. When the time came, palms were opened and all the butterflies flew away—except the one held by the husband. The butterfly stayed in his palm. It wobbled to one of the fingers, then moved back and forth for quite a long time. It was in no hurry to leave. Everyone watched in disbelief and knew that the wife did not want to leave her grieving husband. She loved butterflies and everyone saw this as a sign from her. Finally, the butterfly flew out of the palm of his hand and went directly to the casket, where it landed and remained.

Love doesn't end at "transformation."

Joseph—My Son, My Guide

Please remember that each contact is so personal. It makes no difference if anyone believes you. The message is personal for you, *and you will know.*

This is one of my own experiences. When my father died (transformed to a new life), I wanted a connection. I had worked with him for many years in the jewelry business. We were very close. One night, I asked him to send me a "word" that would be our contact.

The nursery rhyme, "Twinkle, twinkle, little star, . . . like a diamond in the sky," came to mind. I thought, *Of course, diamond is our word.* I decided to experiment by asking Dad to contact me on my birthday. I was open to however it might happen. While watching TV on the evening of my special day, the DeBeers commercial came on: "Diamonds are forever." I started to cry, because I knew it was him.

For several years, on my birthday, I would turn on the TV and expect my contact. I always got it, no matter what channel I was watching.

One year, my daughter was over for my birthday and my television was acting up. I got nothing but fuzzy static. She tried various channels back and forth to no avail. All of a sudden, a commercial popped onto the screen: "Diamonds are forever." Then, immediately, the TV went back to *no* picture, only static for the rest of the night. My dad was determined to wish me a Happy Birthday.

Many such contacts continued in the following years, some in quite unusual ways.

Thoughts and Reflections

When I suffer the loss of someone very close to me, how does my faith help me get through my grieving process?

If I paused to listen and reflect as recommended during this chapter, what did I hear or experience?

What are my thoughts/beliefs about Jesus of Nazareth?

SEASONS OF LIFE

"All I have seen teaches me to trust the creator for all I have not seen." Ralph Waldo Emerson

For several years, messages trickled down to me now and then. Most were of a personal nature, nudging me on, giving me support. I married Sal, the handsome young man who had escorted me to my senior prom, and I gained two more daughters, a son, a daughter-in-law and three more granddaughters.

"My cup runneth over . . ." (Psalm 23:5).

I worked as a real estate agent, continued my grief ministry, and became a *great* grandmother four times. Earth Life was very busy.

In 2012, my messages resumed fast and furious. Evidently, the spirit world felt that this channel was *finally* ready. Talk about patience! Generally, there were no bells, whistles, or beeps. Rather, a "knowing" to get up and write. I let go and decided to surrender to the process. Sometimes, messages came so swiftly that it was hard to keep up. They forced me to invent my own shorthand. There were times when the messages consisted of just a few sentences; yet at other times, it seemed as if I was writing a thesis. But it all worked out.

Here goes:

LIFE ON EARTH IS MAGICAL, FOR THERE IS A SEASON FOR EVERYTHING.

EACH SOUL HAS THEIR OWN SEASON. THE PURPOSE OF LIFE ON EARTH IS TO KNOW HOW TO ATTUNE YOURSELF TO YOUR OWN SEASON AND TRUST THE TIMING FOR EACH EVENT. TO SECOND-GUESS THE TIMING IS TO DELAY THE LESSON OR THE GIFT. ALL IS WELL WHEN YOU STAND IN TRUST.

EVERYONE HAS A PREPARED JOURNEY.
THE SOUL HAS PLANNED WHAT IT NEEDS TO ADVANCE IN KNOWLEDGE AND WISDOM FOR ITS HIGHEST GOOD.

JUDGMENT OF ANOTHER IS FOOLISH.
IT DELAYS YOUR OWN GROWTH ON THE PLANET. EVERYONE HAS THE SPARK WITHIN TO DO WONDROUS THINGS AND MAKE A DIFFERENCE.

THE TIME ON EARTH IS TO STAY FOCUSED ON THIS MISSION AND LET IT UNFOLD THROUGH THE VARIOUS SEASONS OF THE INDIVIDUAL SOUL PURPOSE. WE ARE MANY WHO ASSIST AND GUIDE, WHEN ASKED TO DO SO.

Joseph—My Son, My Guide

A SIMPLE THING, LIKE A SMILE, HAS SUCH ENERGY. BE AN EXAMPLE OF LOVE IN ALL THAT YOU DO AND SAY. SHOW MERCY TO THE UNDESIRABLES, AS OUR GOD SHOWS MERCY TO YOU. BLESS YOUR SITUATION IN THIS MOMENT.

This struck me, because "a smile" can make such a difference. Even a nod or an acknowledgement of some kind, whether you give it or receive it. I have seen eyes light up when I have extended a compliment or acknowledged a person pushing a shopping cart with personal belongings, or given "a little something" that meant, "You matter."

I've also been on the receiving side, when having a low day—a call from an old friend or a stranger saying something pleasant to me while standing in line at the grocery store. We all serve in our own way, and it *all* matters.

SADNESS IS ALSO PART OF LIFE'S JOURNEY. MOVE THROUGH IT KNOWING, BELIEVING AND TRUSTING IT WILL PASS. SADNESS IS ALSO A SEASON. SOMETIMES BRIEF AND OFTEN LONG-LASTING, DEPENDING ON THE LESSON OR THE SOUL'S INTENTION.

IT IS DIFFICULT, YOU MIGHT SAY.
AND WE RESPOND, YES, IT CAN BE.

EMBRACE THE EXPERIENCE AND FEEL THE SENSATIONS. NOT TO KNOW THE SADNESS IS NOT

TO ACKNOWLEDGE IT AS PART OF THE HUMAN EXPERIENCE.

WE STAND WITH YOU DURING THESE CHALLENGING TIMES. YOU ARE IN YOUR PERSONAL SEASON.

I related to the above message. In my grief work, there is a saying I have repeated many times: "I have no magic potion to take away your pain. I wish I did." There is no right way or wrong way to grieve, and it takes as long as it takes.

HOW DIFFICULT CAN BE THE PATH OF CAREGIVERS, COUNSELORS, NURSES, DOCTORS, AND MINISTERS. TO CALM AND GIVE HOPE IS THE ULTIMATE GIFT TO THOSE RECEIVING. NO KIND WORD OR GESTURE IS LOST ON THE RECEIVER. TWO SOULS BLEND TOGETHER, KNOWING THEY ARE ONE.

THE RESULTS ARE OFTEN UNSEEN BUT ALWAYS FELT.
THE HELPER AND THE HELPLESS ARE THE SAME.
ONE HAS BEEN THE OTHER BEFORE.
ALLOW THE ACHE, IF YOU MUST, AND THEN RELEASE TO THE DIVINE PLAN.

℘

EVERY THOUGHT AND ACTION CREATES POWER AND OUTCOME. IT IS A GREAT GIFT WHEN USED WISELY. THINK LOVE, GOODNESS, FAIRNESS, AND COMPASSION AND SEE HOW YOUR LIFE CHANGES. BE THE PERSON YOU WANT TO ATTRACT.

Joseph—My Son, My Guide

THINK THE SITUATION YOU WANT FOR YOURSELF. DO NOT BE LIMITED IN THOUGHT OR DESIRE BY THE CIRCUMSTANCES IN WHICH YOU FIND YOURSELF.

THIS CAN BE USED AS A TEACHER TO MOTIVATE YOU TO REACH INTO YOUR HEART AND THINK OF THE CIRCUMSTANCE YOU DESIRE. YOU HAVE PLANTED THE SEED.

GO ABOUT YOUR BUSINESS. STAY FOCUSED WHILE THE SEED OF YOUR DESIRE IS GROWING. THAT SEED IS YOUR FUTURE.

TREAT IT AS A PRECIOUS BABY. MANIFESTATION OF YOUR HEART'S DESIRE IS EASY, BUT IT TAKES PATIENCE. ALLOW ONLY SUPPORTIVE THOUGHTS TO NOURISH THE SEED OF DESIRE WHICH IS ALREADY ATTRACTING THAT WHICH YOU DESIRE. JUST BE. THAT IS ENOUGH. APPRECIATE THE MOMENT, NO MATTER THE CIRCUMSTANCE GIVEN TO YOU.

IT IS IN THE GRATITUDE THAT MORE APPEARS, WHICH IS WHAT YOU ARE ATTRACTING. EACH SOUL HAS THE SAME CAPACITY TO CREATE. HOWEVER, DO NOT JUDGE ANOTHER SOUL'S JOURNEY.

EVERYONE PLAYS A SIGNIFICANT ROLE. THANK YOU, CHILD, FOR YOUR EAGERNESS TO DELIVER OUR MESSAGES. WE HAVE CHOSEN EACH OTHER. BLESS YOU.

I started to go back to bed, but I heard more dictation:

THERE IS MORE. LOOK INTO THE EYES OF AN

INNOCENT CHILD. THAT IS YOU.

RECAPTURE THAT ZEST FOR THE LITTLE THINGS
THAT BRING YOU JOY. NURTURE YOURSELF AND
REALLY LOOK AT THE WORLD AROUND YOU WITH
NEW CHILDLIKE EYES.
IT'S WONDROUS.
SEE THE CHILD IN EVERYONE.

I must share what happened one morning at about 5:30. I was in a deep sleep when I sensed these words: "You must write this," then the words, "Lemons and Oranges." *I'm dreaming!* I thought, but the words "Lemons and Oranges" came with greater strength and urgency. I was forced to sit up, awakened for yet another lesson. These words poured out:

A LEMON IS A LEMON.

AN ORANGE IS AN ORANGE.

WHAT'S THE DIFFERENCE? BOTH ARE EDIBLE.

ONE APPEALS TO TASTE BUDS, ONE DOES NOT,
AS IT DOESN'T HAVE THE SWEETNESS.

THE SAME APPLIES TO LIFE. WE ARE ATTRACTED TO
THE SWEETNESS, AND YET IT IS THE BITTER THAT
OFTEN PROVIDES THE GREATEST LESSON AND GIFT.
EMBRACE IT ALL.

Thoughts and Reflections

What 'season' of my life am I in?

How challenging is it for me to see blessings in the hardships of my life?

In what sense do I believe that my daily thoughts are creating my future?

PEACE

"To keep a lamp burning, we have to keep putting oil in it."
Mother Teresa

Our planet is in trouble, I know you've heard this from many different sources, but these messages came through, clear and distinct. Other than recycling and trying to buy "green," they give us another way of looking at what our contribution can be.

WE HAVE COME WITH A MESSAGE TO HEAL THE PLANET.

BEGIN WITH YOURSELF.
PRAISE THE CREATOR FOR WHAT HE HAS CREATED.

LOVE THE CREATOR WITHIN YOU.
THE SEED TO HEAL IS WITHIN EACH OF YOU.

LOVE YOUR NEIGHBOR, FOR HE IS YOUR BROTHER, YOUR SISTER, YOUR MOTHER AND YOUR FATHER.
TEACH BY EXAMPLE.

A loud clang from the phone woke me with the following message:

WE GUIDE YOU DAILY. WRITE WHAT WE SAY TO YOU. THE WORLD IS IN DANGER OF DESTRUCTION.

Powerful! But I didn't like hearing this.

℘

PRAY FOR PEACE.
LOVE IS THE ANSWER.
TEACH LOVE.
BE LOVE.

IT CAN BE DONE. MANY HELP.
DO NOT ALLOW FEAR TO MAKE YOU A HOSTAGE.

LOVE ALWAYS WINS, DESPITE THE APPEARANCE OF CONFUSION AND CHAOS.

THANK YOU FOR SHARING THE MESSAGE.
THAT IS ALL, CHILD.

A minute later, I heard:

THERE IS MORE—DOUBT IS AN "ENERGY."

BELIEVE ALL IS POSSIBLE, BECAUSE IT IS.
LOVE AND PRAYER ARE THE ANSWER.

On another morning . . .

Joseph—My Son, My Guide

THERE IS SADNESS ON EARTH TO BE SURE.

DO WHAT YOU CAN TO HELP YOUR BROTHERS
AND SISTERS, BUT DON'T BECOME ANXIOUS,
AS EACH SOUL HAS A JOURNEY.

AGAIN, WE SAY, DON'T BE ANXIOUS. THERE IS A
DIVINE PLAN. YOU CAN ALIGN AND PRAY FOR PEACE
ON THE PLANET. THAT IS YOUR CONTRIBUTION TO
POVERTY AND VIOLENCE.
TO HEAL THE PLANET IS YOUR ROLE IN HELPING ALL
WHO SUFFER.

WHEN THE MASSES COMMIT TO PEACE, ONLY
THEN WILL THERE BE A SHIFT IN THE PLANET.
IT CAN HAPPEN.

I received this clarification . . .

CHILD, OUR WORDS ARE MEANT FOR EVERYONE
WHO IS SEARCHING FOR MEANING.

WE ARE HERE TO SAY EACH ROLE IS IMPORTANT
IN SAVING THE PLANET.
SPEAK OF PEACE.
LIVE PEACE.

BE COMPASSIONATE AND KIND TO ALL. WITHIN EACH
IS THE SEED OF GOD.
WE THANK YOU, CHILD, FOR BRINGING OUR
MESSAGES TO THE WORLD.
THAT IS ALL FOR NOW.

MAY YOU KNOW PEACE. IT IS FREE. ALLOW IT IN YOUR LIFE. YOU HAVE A CHOICE.

TO TRUST GIVES YOU PEACE. TO BELIEVE GIVES YOU PEACE. EACH SOUL HAS THE CAPACITY TO OUTREACH PEACE. SPEAK WITH GENTLE AUTHORITY. CONFIDENCE BRINGS PEACE TO THE BODY, MIND, AND SPIRIT.

ALL HAVE THE DESIRE FOR INNER PEACE, AND WE SAY: QUIET THE MIND. FIND TIME EACH DAY TO SIT IN SILENCE AND PONDER THE *"ALL WHICH IS GOD."*

LET GO OF THE NOISE IN YOUR MIND, THE UNNECESSARY CHATTER. ONLY IN QUIET AND SILENCE DO THE ANSWERS SURFACE AND PEACE FOLLOWS. YOU MAY SAY, THAT SOUNDS SIMPLE; AND WE SAY, *IT IS.*

WE ARE PLEASED WITH YOU.

℘

THE PLANET CAN LIVE IN PEACE, IF EACH BROUGHT ONLY LOVE INTO THEIR TINY SPACE THEY INHABIT. BEGIN TODAY. YOU CAN BE A BEING OF LIGHT IN A SHADOWED WORLD.

DO SOMETHING TODAY FOR SOMEONE, WHICH WILL BRIGHTEN THEIR DAY. IT IS A CIRCLE OF GIVING AND RECEIVING.

THERE IS ENOUGH.

Thoughts and Reflections

What am I doing to help save the planet?

What am I doing to make life better for those with whom I share planet Earth?

LOVE AND PURPOSE

"Ask, and it will be given you. Seek, and you will find; knock, and it will be opened to you." Luke 11:9

The night before I typed the last of my scribbled pages, I received a message that the book was complete. I can't say I was surprised. I had an inner feeling that it had come to a conclusion.

The truth is, I felt a little sad. These messages are so full of *Love*. I appreciate the privilege of sharing them with you and have experienced such serenity and peace while typing them. I feel truly humbled and my tears flow in gratitude.

HELLO, AGAIN.
WE ARE HERE TO SAY, THANK YOU FOR SHARING OUR MESSAGES.

JESUS IS OUR LORD AND SAVIOR.
HIS CHRIST-LIGHT SHINES ON THE WORLD.

BELIEVERS AND NONBELIEVERS TAKE NOTE—

YOU ARE NEVER ALONE.

THE CHRIST-LIGHT OF GOD DWELLS WITHIN EACH
OF YOU. IF YOU ONLY KNEW HOW MUCH
YOU ARE LOVED.
LOVE HEALS. LOVE IS ALL.
EMBRACE YOURSELF, FOR YOU ARE LOVE.

YOU WERE BORN WITH THE GIFT OF UNCON-
DITIONAL LOVE. REMOVE THE SHADOWS THAT KEEP
LOVE FROM SHINING IN YOUR LIFE.

ASK FOR HELP. IT IS THERE FOR THE ASKING.
EVERYTHING IS POSSIBLE WHEN LOVE IS PRESENT.
DOES NOT A TREE BEAR FRUIT, EVEN IF NEGLECTED?
THAT IS LOVE.
LOVE OVERCOMES WHEN ALL SEEMS OR APPEARS
HOPELESS.
THE SPARK IS ALWAYS WITHIN.

BREATHE AND ALLOW THE LOVE OF GOD TO CHANGE
THE NEGLECTED PART OF YOU, THE PART THAT HAS
SHUT OUT THE LOVE.

DON'T DESPAIR. YOUR FRUIT WILL MANIFEST, IF YOU
STEP OUT OF THE WAY AND EMBRACE LOVE.

BECOME FRIENDS WITH YOURSELF.
FERTILIZE YOURSELF BY THINKING GOOD
THOUGHTS, LIVING BY EXAMPLE WHAT LOVE CAN
DO.

IF YOU ONLY KNEW THE POWER OF LOVE, YOUR
LIGHT WOULD BECOME BRILLIANT.
DON'T BE DORMANT.

NOURISH YOURSELF EACH DAY WITH THE LOVE
WHICH IS YOUR INHERITANCE.

YOU MAY SAY, THIS SOUNDS TOO EASY.
IT IS.
WHY LOOK FOR COMPLEXITY, WHEN IT IS SIMPLE.
IT TAKES PRACTICE. BEGIN NOW. BREATHE IN LOVE.
DOESN'T THAT FEEL REFRESHING?

LET LOVE BE YOUR MANTRA, AS YOU MOVE
THROUGH YOUR SOUL JOURNEY.

WE ARE ALL CONNECTED.
WE ARE ONE VIBRATION. THE VIBRATION IS LOVE.
WHEN EACH SOUL FEELS THE CONNECTION, THERE
WILL BE PEACE.

Wow! Close your eyes for a moment and feel all the love in and around you.

You are a beautiful spirit.

(Take a moment to breathe in that love, experience it.)

EACH PERSON HAS GUIDANCE WAITING TO BE
CALLED UPON TO HELP AND OFFER INSIGHT.
ONLY REMEMBER TO ASK. WE ARE HAPPY AND
READY WHEN CALLED UPON.
WE WAIT IN THE WINGS, SO TO SPEAK.
WE ALSO HAVE HUMOR AND RECOMMEND THAT YOU
FIND JOY AND LAUGHTER IN THE LITTLE DAILY
ENCOUNTERS. IT WILL LIGHTEN YOUR LOAD, SO TO
SPEAK.

BALANCE YOUR DAY WITH ALL THAT NOURISHES YOUR PHYSICAL BODY, FOR IT IS YOUR TEMPLE WHICH HOLDS YOUR BRILLIANT SOUL.
TREAT IT WITH DIGNITY. IT IS THE GIFT YOU HAVE CHOSEN.

LOOK BEYOND THE APPEARANCE, FOR IT SERVES YOU. BE THE LIGHT TO THOSE WHO NEED THE LIGHT. SHARE THAT WHICH HAS BEEN GIVEN YOU FREELY FROM THE FATHER.

BEWARE OF JUDGMENT. YOU KNOW NOT ANOTHER'S SOUL JOURNEY. THAT IS ALL FOR NOW, CHILD.

※

You are *never* alone. I can tell you that your guidance is just waiting to be called upon. And yes, they do have humor. Sometimes guidance is firm and stern. When you are in danger, they come *without* being called.

On one of my first trips to Greece, I was foolish to travel alone. At the airport, I shared a taxi cab with a Greek businessman who spoke English, which gave me some confidence. We were both going into Athens. About a mile down the highway, our cab driver pulled over to the right, and another cab pulled in front of him at the side of the highway. The driver of the other taxi came over to us. All three men began speaking in Greek. The way they kept glancing at me, gave me an uneasy feeling.

The man who spoke English asked, "Do you have cash or American Express checks?"

Stunned, I said, "None of your business."

The very next second, a *loud, audible* voice in my head said, "Get out now!"

I still flinch when I recall how I threw open the back door, yanked my roller suitcase out, and started walking fast down the highway.

Behind me, the three men were yelling, "Madam, madam."

With a rapidly beating heart, I came to a roadside café and went in. I did get another ride into Athens, this time with a police officer who was having lunch at the cafe. I had told him my story. My choices, after all, were limited —I could trust him . . . or call another cab!

I'm not sure where that very loud voice telling me to *'get out now'* came from, but it had to be my guardian angel or another guide. Believe me, this was *not* the "inner dictation" I now receive. I was so thankful when I arrived safely at my hotel that I kept repeating, "Thank you." When I finally plopped into my bed that night, I felt so protected.

Yes, we have guidance, even when we don't ask for it.

℘

IT IS TO BE SAID THAT PRAYER WORKS MIRACLES AND IT DOES. A PRAYER IS ALWAYS HEARD AND ALWAYS ANSWERED. THE ANSWER IS ALWAYS FOR THE SOUL'S HIGHEST GOOD. THE BELIEVER KNOWS THIS—ALSO THE UNBELIEVER. HOWEVER, HE HAS FORGOTTEN.
CONTINUE TO PRAY, FOR IT BRINGS THE REMEMBERING CLOSER.
THE FATHER IS PLEASED.

YOU MIGHT ASK, HOW DOES ONE PRAY? SIMPLY ASK FROM THE HEART, SIMPLY SHOW GRATITUDE FROM THE HEART.

EVERY PRAYER IS HEARD, MY CHILD.

BEING AWARE OF THE BEAUTY OF NATURE IS A PRAYER . . . A GOOD GESTURE IS A PRAYER . . . A SMILE TO A STRANGER IS A PRAYER . . . FEEDING THE HUNGRY IS A PRAYER . . . KINDNESS IS A PRAYER.

THE FATHER KNOWS YOUR HEART.
IF IT IS FILLED WITH LOVE, THAT IS A PRAYER.

The above message reminds me of my mother, Rose. Her whole life was a prayer.

The night she passed in 2003, I asked her mentally to send me a contact that she had "arrived." I thought a *rose* sign would be appropriate, since it was her name and Dad always brought her red roses.

Cathi had been with me the night Mom "Ganny" crossed over. She had laid a dozen red roses on her grandmother's pillow, and we told her Dad was waiting for her. Mom's eyes were wide open and she looked at us with such love. Perfect peace filled the room.

Coming back from the memorial reception, those of us in the car glanced to our right as a white van passed with a *red rose* painted on the gas tank flap. I shared with the others that I had asked Mom for a sign. Cathi hadn't been in the same car with us. When I told her about the rose on the gas cap, she was so disappointed.

After hearing my story, Cathi asked Ganny to send her a sign. The very next day, as she parked in front of Walmart, a van parked beside her. It had a *red rose* painted on the door. No writing, no advertising, just a red rose.

My little 4-foot, 11-inch mother is a gentle but powerful soul.

☙

TRUTH IS POWERFUL. ALWAYS COME FROM THAT POSITION.
BE SIMPLE IN THOUGHT AND ELIMINATE THE CLUTTER AND DISTRACTION.
REMEMBER WHY YOU ARE HERE AND TAKE TIME

TO REFLECT.

IN THE STILLNESS OF MIND COMES
THE REMEMBRANCE.

℘

IN EACH OF US, ON EITHER SIDE, IS THE ENORMOUS LOVE OF GOD. IF ONLY YOU KNEW HOW MUCH GOD LOVES US. AGAIN WE SAY, EVERYTHING IS LOVE.

UNDER THE DARKNESS EXPERIENCE IS LOVE.
BELIEVE WITH YOUR HEARTS THAT GOD LOVES YOU UNCONDITIONALLY, WHATEVER YOUR FAULTS.
ALLOW YOURSELF THE LUXURY OF BATHING IN HIS LOVE. ALL ELSE WILL MELT AWAY, AND YOU WILL SEE CLEARLY THE PATH BEFORE YOU.
IN AN INSTANT, CIRCUMSTANCES CAN CHANGE.

WHEN IN DOUBT, REREAD THIS, MY CHILD.

I believe this last statement.

It is powerful.

It is true.

℘

IT IS TIME TO SAY GOODBYE TO OLD WAYS OF THINKING. START ANEW TODAY, AS IF IT WAS THE FIRST DAY OF YOUR EARTH LIFE. ERASE ALL

NEGATIVE INPUT AND SEE WITH THE EYES OF A
NEWBORN. THE BABY REMEMBERS.
GO BACK TO THAT TIME OF REMEMBRANCE . . . PURE
LOVE . . . PURE JOY. . . PURE GRACE.

AS YOU BEGIN YOUR DAY, NOTICE EVERYTHING
AROUND YOU AS IF SEEING IT FOR THE FIRST TIME.
SHIFT YOUR PERCEPTION. IT WILL SWEETEN YOUR
DAY AND YOU WILL BE AMAZED.

THIS IS THE LESSON FOR THE DAY AND FOR THE
REST OF YOUR LIFE.

YOU MAY ASK, WHY?

WE SAY, WHY NOT?

℘

IT IS TO BE SAID THAT LOVE CONQUERS ALL,
AND IT DOES. WE MEAN THE KIND OF LOVE
THAT IS UNCONDITIONAL, A LOVE THAT KNOWS
NO RESTRAINT. WHEN THIS KIND OF LOVE IS
PRESENT, ANYTHING IS POSSIBLE, FOR THERE
ARE NO BARRIERS AND GOD RESIDES. LET DOWN
YOUR GUARD AND LOVE WITH ALL YOUR HEART.
THERE, YOU WILL FIND PEACE.

What is more unconditional than a dog's love for its owner? My friend, Sandi, has had many experiences with her "animal children," as she calls them. Once they have made their transition, she gets little visits from time to time. Here is one of many experiences in her own words:

> I had him cremated and on the little urn engraved in brass in addition to his name, date of birth and death, '*Little Lamb of God*' printed in his memory. Brandy came to see us many times over the years and still does. A week or so after his transition, I woke up one night in bed and the bedroom was pulsating a beautiful shade of gold and was lit up with a beautiful glow. There sitting among my little Maltese and Yorkie on the bed was Brandy and my other two were licking him as he sat with them. It was so beautiful to see them all enjoying each other.

It appears that our precious pets are also embraced by the love of God and experience a joyful afterlife.

℘

TO FULFILL YOUR MISSION, YOU MUST BE DEDICATED. THIS APPLIES TO EVERYONE.

PERSEVERANCE AND DEDICATION ARE NECESSARY TO REMAIN ON ONE'S JOURNEY.

YOU MAY ASK, WHAT IF THE MISSION IS UNKNOWN? AND WE RESPOND AGAIN: TAKE TIME TO MEDITATE.

THE ANSWERS ARE WITHIN, AND THEY WILL SURFACE, OFTEN IN A DREAM.

☙

ABOVE ALL, CHILD, WE ARE UNDER THE MANTLE OF JESUS AND SPEAK ONLY OF LOVE AND FORGIVENESS.

OUR LORD JESUS, THE CHRIST, HAS GIVEN US THE WAY WHILE ON EARTH AND CONTINUES TO LEAD AND TEACH. HIS MISSION IS TO LEAD ALL TO THE ETERNAL FATHER. WE ASSIST IN SPEAKING, AS MANY OF US HAVE HAD EARTH LIVES AND UNDERSTAND THE CHALLENGES OF LIVING ON THE PLANET.

DO NOT BE ANXIOUS, WE SAY TO ALL,
FOR TRUTH AND LOVE WILL PREVAIL.
TAKE THE TIME TO REFLECT AND PONDER.
AS WE HAVE SAID MANY TIMES BEFORE, THE TRUTH LIES WITHIN YOUR SOUL.
YOU WILL REMEMBER WHY YOU HAVE CHOSEN YOUR PATH.

☙

CHILD, THIS IS A MANUAL FOR THOSE WHO ARE WANTING TO REMEMBER. THESE WORDS WILL STIMULATE THEIR INNER KNOWING. THE FOG WILL BE LIFTED AND THEIR MISSION WILL BE MADE CLEAR. WE ARE HERE ONLY TO ASSIST IN THE PROCESS.

WE SPEAK ONLY LOVE AND TRUTH.

DID NOT JESUS SPEAK OF LOVE AND TRUTH?

☙

ABOVE ALL, REMEMBER TO THANK GOD EACH AND EVERY DAY. GRATITUDE IS THE HIGHEST FORM OF PRAYER.

And so it is . . . .

APPENDIX I

My Answered Prayers

> *"He will wipe every tear from their eyes.*
> *There shall be no more death or mourning, crying out or pain,*
> *for the world that was has passed away."*
> Revelations 21:4

A year after Joseph was born, I was pregnant again. This time, I had a premonition that I would die during childbirth.

When my first child, Bob, was about one year old, I visited a girlfriend who also had a child that age. I remember saying to her, "I have a feeling I'm going to die in childbirth some day." After uttering those words, I wondered, *Why did I say that?*

I never thought of it again, until my *fifth* pregnancy, when the thought of dying resurfaced (Cathi was my second; Mary Ann, stillborn, my third; and Joseph, my fourth). This terrifying thought stayed with me constantly.

I told no one. Saying it out loud might make it real. Day and night, I prayed to Mother Mary and St. Anthony to intercede for me. Reaching out to Jesus' mother and one of his beloved saints came naturally. It was a Catholic thing.

Bob was seven and Cathi, five. Each night, after they were asleep, I would look at them and dread the thought of not raising them. It was a most difficult time. My little secret held me hostage. About three weeks before my scheduled C-section, I went into labor, and the doctor prepared me for emergency surgery. I was 25 years old.

I remember waking up and seeing my mother and my husband, Sam. I glanced to my left and on the nightstand was a yellow chrysanthemum plant with a statue of St. Anthony in the middle of it. My first thought: "I'm alive!" Sam and Mom shared with me what had happened. My baby son had lived several hours, before dying. Because I was bleeding so heavily, they said, the doctor had to perform a hysterectomy to save my life. I tried to absorb what they were saying, but I was still a bit "out of it."

Not knowing who had sent the plant, I asked Mom to

Joseph—My Son, My Guide

read the card to me. It was from an acquaintance who worked at the hospital. We had gone to high school together, but had not been in contact for many years.

Neither she nor anyone else knew of my plea to St. Anthony. It was unbelievable that she would send me a plant with his statue. To this day, I don't even know if she was Catholic. I named my son Anthony.

Since 1960, that statue has sat on my kitchen counter (in many different homes), as a reminder that I was granted my heartfelt prayer. The bonus is that I have lived to see both my son and daughter become grandparents! Now, *that's* a miracle!

And I lived to channel this book.

APPENDIX II

Beyond Words

Only once, while in prayer, was I graced with a message from Mother Mary—a blessing beyond words.

I AM THE PATH THAT LEADS TO THE WAY. HE, JESUS, IS *THE WAY*.

☙

Regarding Mary, let me relate an experience that happened to my good friend, June. She called me in shocked excitement one morning. She had opened her drapes and looked out to a clear sky with only one very large smoky gray cloud. She had to blink twice because as she looked again, the cloud was actually Mother Mary in every detail of form, dress, even to the way her arms hung gently down. She said the experience lasted about 10 minutes.

When she turned away for just a moment, the image disappeared.

To this day, June remembers exactly how Mary looked and feels blessed to have had this "unexpected miracle."

AFTERWORD

Reading this completed manuscript cover to cover is like reading about someone else's experience . . . yet it's my story.

My wish for you is that these messages will inspire you to listen to *your* "inner voice." You are here for a reason. You are significant. Embrace the wonderful spiritual being that you are, and EXPECT MIRACLES!

Joseph and The Many have told me, "We will work together again."

I'm not certain what that will entail, but I am now a willing and grateful channel. I trust God's plan.

Joseph—My Son, My Guide

Gazing Above

by

Alison Joy King

Trying to look beyond what meets the eye
A perfectly white moon
With one glistening star floating there beside it
Thin streaks of pinkish clouds
Randomly spotting the midnight sky
We didn't even know each other . . .
A breeze passes,
Only leaving goose bumps as its footprints
My mind feeling hollow,
And yet completely cluttered
Where is your presence?
Listening carefully to the silence of the night
I've lost count of the hours I've spent

Simply searching for a sign
That you've made it to your destination
If I had a chance to give you a message . . .
A better place
Fitting your wonders, I'm sure
Dancing in the heavens,
At this moment exact
Are you watching the life you left behind . . . ?
You changed this world
Are you aware?
Causing all of us to come together
Are you surprised?
All eyes and hearts pointed towards the sky,
sending only our truest love
Can you feel it?
Every soul touched forever
Are you watching?
So many wonders arise,
Simply from gazing above.

ABOUT THE AUTHOR

Kathryn Davi-Cardinale is a certified grief counselor and clinical hypnotherapist. She and her husband, Sal, live in the San Francisco Bay Area. You are invited to contact the author at *joseph.myguide@gmail.com*.

KINDRED SPIRITS

Deborah Brooks
www.deborahbrooks.com

Alfred J. Garrotto
algarrotto@comcast.net
www.alfredjgarrotto.com
www.wisdomoflesmiserables.blogspot.com
www.saintofflorenville.com
[The novel, *The Saint of Florenville: A Love Story*, has been optioned for production as a feature film.]

Franci Lucero
(925) 228-4338
www.photosbyfranci.com

Joanne Macko
www.angelic-art.com
(650) 579-8184

Shirley Ruiz-Orlich
Quantum Angel Network
www.quantumangel.net

Kay Taylor
www.kaytaylor.com
(925) 932-3331

Additional Thoughts, Reflections, and Insights

Made in the USA
San Bernardino, CA
22 February 2018